THE CLASSICS OF WESTERN SPIRITUALITY
A Library of the Great Spiritual Masters

President and Publisher
Kevin A. Lynch, C.S.P.

EDITORIAL BOARD

FAKHRUDDIN 'IRAQI

DIVINE FLASHES

TRANSLATION AND INTRODUCTION
BY
WILLIAM C. CHITTICK and
PETER LAMBORN WILSON

PREFACE
BY
SEYYED HOSSEIN NASR

PAULIST PRESS
NEW YORK • RAMSEY • TORONTO

Cover Art
The artist, WILL HARMUTH, is a professional artist and illustrator who lives in Bernardsville, New Jersey. A graduate of Newark School of Fine/Industrial Arts, Mr. Harmuth also attended the Arts Students League.

Library of Congress
Catalog Card Number: 82-80859

ISBN: 0-8091-0329-X (cloth)
        0-8091-2372-X (paper)

Published by Paulist Press
545 Island Road, Ramsey, N.J. 07446

Printed and bound in the
United States of America

Contents

WILLIAM CLARK CHITTICK was born in Milford, Connecticut, in 1943.
He received his B.A. in history at the College of Wooster in Ohio in 1966 and
became interested in Sufism and Islamic philosophy during his junior year at
the American University of Beirut. Upon graudation from Wooster he went
to Tehran to enroll in the Ph.D. program for Persian language and literature
with the aim of acquiring the necessary tools to study Islamic thought. In
Tehran his studies were guided by Seyyed Hossein Nasr, with whom he later
collaborated on a number of projects. After finishing his Ph.D., he taught
comparative religion, history and courses dealing with the problems of traditional and modern societies at Aryamehr Technical University in Tehran.
(All courses were taught in Persian.) Dr. Chittick collaborated in several of
the projects being carried out at the newly founded Imperial Iranian Academy of Philosophy and began teaching Sufi philosophy and metaphysics there
in 1978. He is the author of a number of articles and books including *The Sufi
Doctrine of Rumi: An Introduction and A Shiᶜite Anthology*. The Chitticks left Iran
in 1979 just prior to the revolution.

PETER WILSON was born near Baltimore, Maryland in 1945. After studying at Columbia University, he did extensive traveling in the Middle East,
Afghanistan, Pakistan, India and Nepal. He studied Tantra in West Bengal
and visited many Sufi shrines and masters. In 1971 he undertook research on
the Ni' matullahi funded by the Marsden Foundation of New York. This re-
sulted in his publication of *Kings of Love: The History and Poetry of the Ni' matullahi Sufi Order of Iran*, with N. Pourjavadui; Tehran, 1978. During 1974 and
1975 he was consultant in London and Tehran for the World of Islam Festi-
val. In 1974 he became director of English language publications at the Imperial Iranian Academy of Philosophy in Tehran under Seyyed Hossein Nasr,
and he studied, worked with, and published books by Nasr, Toshihiko,
Izutsu, Henry Corbin and others. He was editor of *Sophia Perennis*, the Jour-
nal of the IIAP. Wilson has published two books of his own poems: *The Winter Calligraphy of Ustad Selin* (Ipswich, England, 1975); and DIVAN (London/
Tehran, 1978).

SEYYED HOSSEIN NASR was born in Tehran in 1933, where he received
his early education. Later he pursued his more advanced studies in America,
first studying physics at M.I.T. and later the history of science and philosophy at Harvard University where he received his Ph.D. in 1958. He taught
for many years at Tehran University, was the first holder of the chair of Islamic studies at the American University of Beirut, and Visiting Professor at
Harvard University. He has also lectured extensively throughout the world
and delivered the Gifford Lectures in 1981 at the University of Edinburgh.
Nasr is an international authority on Islam and especially Sufism and author
of over twenty books of which many are devoted to subjects related to Islamic
spirituality, including *Ideals and Realities of Islam* and *Sufi Essays*. Since 1979 he
has been professor of religion at Temple University.

Preface

The Sufi tradition is like a vast garden in which are cultivated many flowers of different scents and colors, each sweet and beautiful, each reflecting one aspect of the garden of paradise, and each with its own particular form. There are certain Sufi writings that are primarily practical and operative, others that express the metaphysical and cosmological doctrines of the tradition, and yet another group that makes use of parables to convey the message of Sufism. Moreover, although the inner reality of Sufism is everywhere the same, containing and reflecting the very heart of the Islamic message, its modes of expression have taken into consideration the artistic possibilities of the peoples whom they have addressed and the genius of the languages they have employed.

In this garden of divine mysteries, there have appeared certain flowers whose perfume has filled the world and been appreciated for centuries in lands near and far. One of them is Fakhruddin 'Iraqi (often referred to as 'Araqi) whose prose masterpiece, the *Lama'at* [Divine flashes], appears for the first time in English in this volume. A Persian poet born in the ancient city of Hamadan, he spent some years in India, especially in the city of Multan (which is now in Pakistan), as well as in Konya and Toqat in present-day Turkey. His fame spread over the eastern lands of Islam even during his own lifetime and his writings have been a favorite among devotees of Sufi literature wherever the Persian language has been read or spoken, from Turkey to India. He is known as one of the foremost expositors of Sufi teachings, one of the greatest of Persian poets, and a supreme artist among those who have attained an exalted station of spiritual realization within the Sufi tradition.

'Iraqi lived during the seventh/thirteenth century at the peak of the revival of Islamic spirituality, a time that is like the echo of the

PREFACE

opening century of Islam. He was contemporary with such giants of Sufism as Ibn 'Arabi, Jalaluddin Rumi, Sadruddin Qunawi, Najmuddin Kubra, and Abu'l-Hasan ash-Shadhili, men whose teachings dominate Islamic spirituality to this day. He himself was a leading light in a period so luminous that its brilliance still dazzles the eye some seven centuries later.

'Iraqi, like many of the well-known Sufi masters, was highly educated in both the theological and literary disciplines. He knew well not only the Holy Koran, *hadith*, commentary, *Kalam* (theology), and the like, but also Persian and Arabic literature, particularly the works of earlier Sufis. His many references to such figures as Bayazid, al-Hallaj, Abu'l-Hasan Kharraqani, Sana'i, and others testify to his intimate knowledge of earlier Sufi writings; and his continuous references to the Holy Koran and *hadith* demonstrate his remarkable familiarity with the written sources of the Islamic tradition.

Not only because of his formal education but also as a result of his own personal gift as a poet and a writer, 'Iraqi was drawn to a careful study of Persian literature, one of whose most celebrated figures he himself was destined to become. He knew the earlier poets thoroughly, and from the point of view of form, symbolism, and texture of poetry belongs to the main tradition of Persian Sufi poetry. Before him Persian Sufi poetry had already been developed considerably by such masters as Abu Sa'id Abi'l-Khayr, Sana'i, and 'Attar. In fact 'Iraqi was contemporary with the figure who brought this Sufi poetical tradition to its peak, namely Jalaluddin Rumi. To understand the language of 'Iraqi, it is necessary to consider his intimate relationship with this school of Persian Sufi poetry to which he himself belongs.

But 'Iraqi was also closely associated with another school of Sufism, which is identified with the name of Muhyiuddin ibn 'Arabi, and was thoroughly versed in the gnostic and metaphysical teachings of this school. 'Iraqi was at once a metaphysician of the Ibn 'Arabian school of Sufism and an artist of the Persian school of Sufism that was to culminate with Rumi. 'Iraqi can be considered a member of the small group of eminent Persian Sufis, including Awhaduddin Kirmani and 'Abdurrahman Jami, who belonged to both worlds. The letter of 'Iraqi to Sadruddin Qunawi, discovered by W. Chittick and translated for the first time in this volume, attests to the close link between 'Iraqi and the school of Ibn 'Arabi, for it must be remembered that Sadruddin was the foremost expositor of the teachings of Ibn

PREFACE

'Arabi and the person through whom the doctrines of the Andalusian master reached most of the Islamic world, especially the eastern areas.

The spiritual training of 'Iraqi, as of every adept of Sufism, was of course not through literature or even formal religious education. It was through initiation and spiritual discipline, as is shown in the Life in the present volume. Everything else followed from that fundamental and central training, which aimed at the purification of the heart, the goal that is basic to Sufism. 'Iraqi *became* a work of art before producing works of art. If he sang the love of God in verses of great beauty, it is because his soul had itself become a song of God, a melody in harmony with, and a strain of, the music issuing from the abode of the Beloved.

'Iraqi was a gnostic who spoke in the language of love. For him, as for Sufism in general, love is not juxtaposed to knowledge. It is *realized* knowledge. The Truth, which is like a crystal or a shining star in the mind, becomes wine when it is lived and realized. It inundates the whole of man's being, plucking the roots of his profane consciousness from this world of impermanence and bringing about an inebriation that must of necessity result from the contact between the soul of man and the infinite world of the Spirit. But 'Iraqi was a Sufi gifted particularly in expressing the "mysteries of Union" in the language of love. He belongs to that group of Sufis, like Ruzbahan Baqli, the patron saint of Shiraz, who have been called the *fideli d'amore* of Islam.

More specifically, the *Lama'at* of 'Iraqi belongs to a particular type of Sufi literature in which the purest doctrines of gnosis (*al-ma'rifah*) were expressed in the language of love (*al-mahabbah*). The first work of this kind in Persian literature is the *Sawanih fi'l-'ishq* [*Spark of Love*] of Ahmad Ghazzali, the brother of the better-known Abu Hamid Muhammad Ghazzali. This remarkable literary and spiritual masterpiece was followed by the *Risalah fi haqiqat al-'ishq* [*Treatise on The Reality of Love*] by the founder of the school of illumination, Shihabuddin Suhrawardi. The *Lama'at* of 'Iraqi is the third major work in this *genre* of Sufi writing and shares in every way the great beauty of its predecessors. There are in fact some who claim that the *Lama'at* is the most beautiful work of its kind in Persian literature. This work became so celebrated in both Persia and India that it served as the inspiration for several later treatises in both countries and was commented on by no less a figure than 'Abdurrahman Jami.

In Islamic thought, the traditional authorities speak of "transcendence" (*tanzih*) and "immanence" (*tashbih*), or the "negative" and "positive" ways, of which the second corresponds more to the perspective of 'Iraqi. He and Sufis like him see the phenomenal world not as the "veil," but rather as the mirror reflecting God's Names and Qualities, or as a symbol of the spiritual world. For them beauty is not the cause of seduction, but the occasion for recollection of the spiritual archetypes in the Platonic sense. Of course God is transcendent and one must renounce and leave the finite in order to reach Him. But He is also immanent. Therefore, when man has passed through the stage of renunciation and separation from the world of forms for the sake of the Formless, it is possible for him to return to forms as the mirror of the Formless. But this can happen only if the first stage—that of renunciation, asceticism, and separation from the world—has been experienced. For as Frithjof Schuon has stated, "It is not possible to experience God as the Immanent without having experienced Him as the Transcendent." But having experienced Him as the Transcendent, it is possible in Sufi spirituality, as in most other authentic traditions, to become aware of the metaphysical transparency of forms and to be able to contemplate the One in the multifaceted manifold.

It is this perspective that makes possible a "spiritualized sensuality" that is very different from the dualism that would totally oppose the spirit to the flesh and mind to matter. This is a compartmentalization from which many modern Westerners suffer as a result of a complex set of historical factors, including of course Cartesian dualism, which has constructed an impenetrable wall between "mind" and "matter." This philosophical dualism has furthermore become fortified by a kind of religious dualism that also sees a total and final opposition between the spirit and the flesh, as if there were no doctrine of the resurrection of the body, in Christianity as in Islam. The result of these factors has been the spread of a kind of religious mentality for which it would be difficult to imagine how a person with serious spiritual intentions could talk in sensuous terms, employing continuously the image of wine or human beauty.

To understand the point of view of an 'Iraqi, it is necessary to transcend this dichotomy and to return to the more traditional perspective, which is also present in certain schools of Western spirituality. In the perspective of an 'Iraqi there is no irreducible dichotomy between divine and human love or divine and human beauty. There is a gradation from the love of forms, which is "apparent love" (*'ishq-i*

PREFACE

majazi), to the love of God, which alone is "real love" (*'ishq-i haqiqi*). The lower form of love can be, and for the Sufi *is*, the ladder to Divine Love. Ultimately, to love anything is to love God, once man realizes that there is but One Love. Likewise, there is a gradation of beauty from formal, human, and terrestrial beauty to Absolute Beauty Itself, the "Beautiful" (*al-jamil*) being a Name of God. In a profounder sense all beauty is like a drop that has fallen from the Divine Cup upon this world of clay. It thus brings about recollection; it frees and saves. For the soul of the gnostic, beauty is like fresh air without which one would die in the suffocating space of the world of limitation.

For 'Iraqi and the *fideli d'amore* of Islam, the beauty of anything can lead to an awareness of the beauty of God, but it is human beauty that is the most direct manifestation of Divine Beauty, for, according to the famous *hadith*, "God created man upon His own image." The theomorphic nature of man is the metaphysical basis for the central role that human beauty plays in certain forms of spiritual contemplation in Sufism and in the type of Sufi poetry for which not only 'Iraqi but also Ibn 'Arabi himself and such later Persian Sufi poets as Hafiz and Jami are famous. A Westerner reading 'Iraqi should think not so much of the pietistic or puritanical writings of the post-medieval period, but of the spiritual universe of a Solomon who in his *Song* could say,

> How fair and how pleasant art thou,
> > O love, for delights!
> This thy stature is like to a palm tree,
> > and thy breasts to clusters of grapes.
> I said, I will go up to the palm tree,
> > I will take hold of the bows thereof:
> now also thy breasts shall be as clusters of the vine,
> > and the smell of thy nose like apples;
> and the roof of thy mouth like the best wine
> > for my beloved, that goeth down sweetly,
> > causing the lips of those that are asleep to speak. (7:6–9)

This type of spirituality is based on seeing the seal of the Logos on manifested forms and on integrating all that is positive in the manifested order in the process of transcending and going beyond all manifestation.

PREFACE

The *Lama'at* is at once a metaphysical treatise and a work of art. It is therefore fortunate that the present edition has been prepared by two men who combine the talents of a scholar and a poet together. William Chittick has spent years in the study of Sufism, particularly the school of Ibn 'Arabi. He has written some of the most scholarly and metaphysically penetrating studies of the followers of Ibn 'Arabi, especially Sadruddin Qunawi and 'Abdurrahman Jami. Peter Wilson is an accomplished poet and is experienced in the translation of Sufi poetry. Moreover, both men have been deeply immersed in Persian culture and have firsthand knowledge of the tradition that gave birth to 'Iraqi. They have been able to combine their efforts to present a volume that will doubtlessly appeal to both the metaphysically and philosophically trained student of religion and spirituality and the person who is more sensitive to the literary and poetic expression of spirituality. In any case their combined efforts make accessible in a manner that is satisfactory at once from the point of view of scholarship and literature one of the most precious pearls of Sufism. Above all, their intimacy with the tradition that has given birth to this work and their traditional point of view are a guarantee of the authentic presentation of this work at a time when unadulterated and genuine studies of Sufism and other forms of Oriental spirituality are so direly needed in the West. Their considerable effort has woven a complex tapestry into a unifed pattern and created a work whose close reading cannot but bring the reader to the words of 'Iraqi himself:

> Before this there was one heart
> but a thousand thoughts.
> Now all is reduced to
> *There is no god but God.*

Seyyed Hossein Nasr
Woodbury, Connecticut
May 26, 1980

Foreword

This book can be approached in two different ways. If the reader is interested primarily in poetry, and is not very familiar or concerned with speculative or philosophical Sufism, he may wish to begin by reading only the Life of 'Iraqi, and then the translation of the text of *Divine Flashes*. If, however, he wishes to follow more closely the speculative background of the work, he should read the Mystical Philosophy and the Life, and then, after reading each chapter or Flash of the text, he should turn to the relevant portion of the Commentary at the end of the book.

In the translated portions of the Life and in the more poetic sections of the text, we have used a somewhat freer approach; while in the Mystical Philosophy and Commentary, and in the more philosophical portions of the text, we have made use of a somewhat more technical and literal style. On the whole, however, and especially in the text itself, we have tried to "trans-create" as well as translate; that is, to offer something that will stand on its own as a work of English literature, and that will provide a more exact rendition of 'Iraqi's *meaning* than a merely literal translation could attain.

In translating the text we made use of the newest and best edition, that of Jawad Nurbakhsh.[1] We collated this with the text provided in *Ashi''at al-lama'at* [Gleams from the flashes],[2] a commentary on 'Iraqi's work written by 'Abdurrahman Jami (d. 898/1492), the great Sufi poet and philosopher. In a few instances we preferred Jami's reading and interpretation to that provided by the Nurbakhsh edition (which also has a number of bad typographical errors). The Life is largely translated from the earliest and most reliable account of 'Iraqi that has come down to us; although tinged with hagiography, it accurately reflects the personality revealed in 'Iraqi's works. The commentary on *Lama'at* is our own, although we have often made use of Jami's remarks to explain individual passages.[3]

FOREWORD

original. Many other quotations are attributed to Sufis or poets for whom we have not thought it necessary to give dates or other biographical data, since they are well known and can be found described in such works as A. J. Arberry's translation of Fariduddin 'Attar's *Tadhkirat al-awliya*'.[4]

NOTES

1. *Risala-yi lama'at wa risala-yi istilahat* (Tehran, 1353/1974).
2. *Ashi''at al-lama'at-i Jami*, ed. H. Rabbani (Tehran, 1352/1973).
3. After completing the work, we had an opportunity to go over a manuscript of an earlier commentary, the *Lamahat* of 'Ala'uddin Yar-'ali Shirazi (fl. second half of eighth/fourteenth c.; ms. Şehid Ali Paşa 1257). We were interested to see that he, far more than Jami, makes use of the works of Qunawi, Farghani, and also Jandi to explain 'Iraqi's ideas. In style, then, our own commentary is more similar to Shirazi's than to Jami's.
4. A. J. Arberry, *Muslim Saints and Mystics* (Chicago, 1966).

Introduction

I The Mystical Philosophy of the Divine Flashes

Islam's fundamental teaching declares: "There is no god but God." Throughout Islamic history practically every school of thought has sought to elucidate this teaching in its own way. In general the theologians (*mutakallimun*) based their explications of God's Oneness on the evidence—incontrovertible in their eyes—provided by the Koran and the *Hadith* of the Prophet. The Peripatetic philosophers (*mashsha'iyyun*) tried to prove God's Unity by appealing to the powers of man's intellect (*'aql*) and the data provided by his sense perception. But the Sufis added a third source of knowledge to the above two: direct vision of the realities of things, or mystical "unveiling" (*kashf*), which is also referred to as "contemplation" (*shuhud, mushahadah*) and "direct-perception" (*dhawq*).[1] In their view, unveiling is incomparably more reliable than the unaided intellect, which can never attain true certainty concerning any matter of lasting importance, in other words, concerning God or man's ultimate end. But at the same time unveiling must be based on revelation and cannot gainsay it. Most Sufis were careful to warn their followers against anyone who ever said or did anything that contradicted the fundamental teachings of the Islamic revelation, even if he should claim divine inspiration and produce "miracles" in support of his claim.[2]

The intermediate position adopted by the Sufis, in which intellect was subordinate to unveiling and unveiling to revelation, is clearly represented by the teachings of the School of Ibn al-'Arabi. Ibn al-'Arabi himself often chooses a mode of expression that makes one think he is claiming a source of inspiration above even the authority of the Koran, although in other places in his own works he modifies this position by insisting on the supreme authority of the Koran and the Prophet. Moreover, his followers, especially his successor and

3

INTRODUCTION

spiritual heir, Sadruddin Qunawi—'Iraqi's master—clearly situate Ibn al-'Arabi's teachings within the hierarchy referred to above. And later Sufis have invariably seen Ibn al-'Arabi through Qunawi's eyes.[3]

These considerations help to explain the peculiar method Sufis like 'Iraqi employ to explain the nature and consequences of God's Oneness. 'Iraqi does not set out to write a Peripatetic exposition or to appeal to the reader's intellect—even though the logical consistency of *Lama'at* shows that he does not ignore the rational faculty. Rather, his explication of God's nature and man's relation to it is based primarily on the intermediate domain specific to the Sufis, that of mystical unveiling, direct-perception and spiritual intuition. But the ultimate authority of the Koran and *Hadith* is never forgotten.

In discussing God's Oneness, the various schools of Islamic thought employ a variety of terms to refer to the Ultimate and Unique Reality. The theologians speak about "God" (*Allah*) and in Koranic terms explain the nature of His Names and Attributes and His relation with the world and man. The Peripatetic philosophers call the Ultimate Reality the "Necessary Being" (*wajib al-wujud*). The Illuminationist philosophers refer to the Ultimate Reality as "Light" (*nur*). The Sufis use innumerable terms, most of them Koranic and most of them immediately identifiable as Divine Names.

As for the particular Sufi school of Ibn al-'Arabi, it also employs numerous terms, including "*Allah*" and "Truth" (*haqq*), although each term it uses has a particular technical connotation. Among the most important of these terms is "Being," the same word employed in the Peripatetic formulation "Necessary Being." So important is this term in Ibn al-'Arabi's teaching that his school is usually referred to as that of the "Oneness of Being" (*wahdat al-wujud*). His disciple Qunawi amplifies and refines Ibn al-'Arabi's teachings on Being's Oneness and in the process begins to bridge the gap between them and those of the Peripatetics.

As for 'Iraqi, he follows—to use his own words—"the tradition of the *Sparks* (*Sawanib*)." In this Persian work, Ahmad Ghazzali (d. 520/1126), the younger brother of the more famous theologian and Sufi Abu Hamid Ghazzali, states that the Ultimate Reality is "Love" (*'ishq, mahabbah*), and on the basis of this statement constructs a complex metaphysics.[4]

The very fact that Ghazzali concerns himself primarily with metaphysics should be enough to alert the reader that in Ghazzali's

4

INTRODUCTION

view, the statement "God is Love" does not carry the usual sentimental or emotional overtones. He draws conclusions that would seem peculiarly intellectual to most Christians who hold the same belief. In spite of certain appearances, his "mysticism" is basically one of knowledge, not of love as usually understood.[5]

Numerous Sufis followed Ghazzali in speaking of God as Love, among them 'Iraqi. But 'Iraqi did not follow the terminological details of Ghazzali's metaphysics, only his identification of God with Love; and as with Ghazzali, 'Iraqi's teachings are based purely on a contemplative vision of the realities of things. When 'Iraqi discusses the nature of Love, he displays a profound comprehension of the metaphysical teachings of his own master, Qunawi. But by identifying God with Love throughout the work, and by employing the same sort of mixed Persian prose and poetry that Ghazzali uses, 'Iraqi is able to state quite correctly that he is following the tradition laid down by Ghazzali.

But the fact that 'Iraqi follows Qunawi's teachings means that his use of the word Love is not just a question of terminology. It is not as if he decides to call God "Love" and to leave everything else the same. True, often it would be sufficient to change "Love" to "Being" in 'Iraqi's sentences to produce statements identical to those of Ibn al-'Arabi's followers who preserved the master's terminology. But this is not always the case. For Ibn al-'Arabi has teachings about Love *qua* Love, which are in turn dealt with extensively by Qunawi and 'Iraqi.

So 'Iraqi's discussion represents a synthesis of two slightly different points of view. In one respect Love is identical with God or Being, as in Ghazzali's *Sparks*. In another respect Love is one of God's Attributes, as in Qunawi's teachings. But even in Qunawi's teachings these two points of view can be combined into one, for if Love in one respect is an Attribute of God, in another respect it is identical with His very Essence. It is God Himself. For, as Qunawi maintains, "The Attributes are in one respect the very Essence Itself. . . . They are the very same as the Essence in the sense that nothing exists there but the Essence. But they are different from the Essence in the sense that the concepts understood from the Essence are definitely different from one another."[6]

In short, 'Iraqi discusses the Oneness of Being in terms of Love. He emphasizes that Being and Love are the same thing, for every Attribute of God is only the Essence viewed from a certain point of view. But the existence of that point of view means that Love can be spoken of in a language peculiar to itself, for that point of view is different from any other.

'Iraqi's originality, then, is that he follows Ghazzali in calling Ultimate Reality "Love," and thus he neglects the terminology relating to the discussion of Being preferred by most of the other members of Ibn al-'Arabi's school. At the same time, almost everything he says about Love—not to speak of Love *qua* Being—is derived from the teachings of his master, Qunawi. But nowhere does his master, nor any of the other followers of Ibn al-'Arabi, succeed in presenting a discussion of Love in such a delightful and readable manner.

So 'Iraqi is discussing the Divine Unity, or the Oneness of Being, in a language peculiar to discussions of love. To clarify these remarks further, it is necessary to explain what Ibn al-'Arabi and his followers mean by the "Oneness of Being," and what they have had to say about Love's relation to Being. How is it that Love is an Attribute of God, and as such, identical with His very Essence?

THE ONENESS OF BEING

"Being is One." This sentence is a constant refrain in Qunawi's writings. To explain its meaning and implications in any detail and in the overall context of Qunawi's works would be far beyond the scope of the present introduction.[7] Here we can only hope to summarize his teachings in the barest outline.

"Being" is that which, by its very nature, *is*. It cannot not be. As for what exactly is meant by this term "to be," on the one hand its meaning is self-evident, and on the other, it is almost impossible to grasp. Everyone has an immediate intuition of what it means for something to "be" or to "exist." In fact, nothing can be closer to our experience and knowledge. The Sufis would emphasize that "I only think because I *am*." In any case, everyone grasps immediately the difference between the existence of something and its nonexistence. Otherwise, there would be no difference between having something and not having it.

But at the same time, almost no one truly grasps the fundamental nature of this "is-ness." Unless it is accompanied by some object or thing, no one can comprehend it. Everyone knows what is meant by "the pencil exists," or that the common measure between "the pencil exists" and "the galaxy exists" is their existence or is-ness. But remove all pencils and galaxies, all objects and entities. What then is meant by is-ness as such? What can it mean that we have defined *being* as "that which, by its very nature, is," when there is no definable thing that is? How can one comprehend this sort of is-ness when it does not correspond to any object whatsoever?

According to Ibn al-'Arabi and his followers, that being which by its very nature *is*, and cannot not be, is "nonentified" (*ghayr muta'ayyan*) or indeterminate. We cannot truly name or describe it. Whatever we describe as possessing such and such an attribute, we define, delimit, and determine. We make it identical to some entity. But being as such—Being—is nonentified and indeterminate. It has no description or delimitation. It is no particular *thing*, not even that "thing" which we usually call "God," that is, as a Reality distinct and separate from the world.

How do we know that Being is nonentified? Because every entity that has being, every thing that exists, is a delimitation of Being as such. We say, "The horse *is*, the tree *is*, Tom *is*, the devil *is*, God *is*." The common measure is is-ness. Nor is this is-ness a mental construct. Rather, it is the fundamental nature of all things.[8] Each entity, each thing, each existent, is one possibility of "entification" (*ta'ayyun*) hidden within the nature of Sheer Being, just as each color is one possibility of "coloration" possessed by the very essence of pure light.[9]

If Being is to assume every single entification and delimitation, in Itself it must be nonentified. It must be able to manifest Itself in every form.[10] For if It were large and only large, nothing small could exist. If It were the Creator and only the Creator, there would be no creatures. These points are summarized in the axiom "Each entification must be preceded by nonentification."[11] Every existent entity or thing derives from a source that in relation to it is indeterminate and

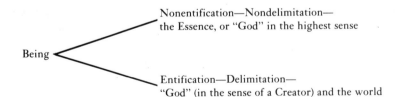

Being —
Nonentification—Nondelimitation—
the Essence, or "God" in the highest sense

Entification—Delimitation—
"God" (in the sense of a Creator) and the world

FIGURE 1: PRELIMINARY DIVISION OF BEING AS SUCH

7

nonentified. Thus a "horse" is an entification of "animal." If animal were by its very nature horse, there could be no dogs or lions. So the entification "horse" is preceded by the relative nonentification "animal." In a similar way, the entification "animal" is preceded by the relative nonentification, "living corporeal-body." But if all living corporeal-bodies were animals, there could be no plants. Finally, when we reach Being Itself, we reach absolute Nonentification, so there can be nothing beyond it. Moreover, since Being is absolutely Nonentified, all entifications are forms It may assume.

Nonentified Being is none other than the Essence (*dhat*) of God. To answer the question "Why does God create the 'world?' (*al-'alam* = "everything other than God")"; or, moving back to a second question implied in the first, "Why does the Essence of God, Nonentified Being, become entified as God the Creator and His creation?" we must investigate more carefully the nature of Being as such.

Being in Itself is Nonentified, and consequently nondelimited, inarticulated, without name, attribute, or quality. So It cannot be described in positive terms. It is Unknown. But as soon as Being assumes any entification, that entification can be described (see Figure 1). Now these entifications are not accidental. The very nature of Being Itself demands that It possess certain "Perfections" or "Possibilities of Self-Manifestation" or "Potentialities" in keeping with which entification will take place. For Being is the source of all things, and therefore also of all properties, laws, and regularities. It has Its own order, rhythm, and modes. It reveals Itself—becomes entified—only in keeping with Its own nature, a nature that possesses certain concomitants and properties that are reflected in all things. These concomitants or ontological perfections are summarized in God's "Names and Attributes" (*asma' wa sifat*), which are Being's universal entifications. The Names and Attributes divide the infinite possible entifications of Being into a number of universal categories. Thus the basic Attributes are Life, Knowledge, Will, and Power. The Attributes are also divided into the "99" or "1001" Divine Names.

But ultimately, since Being is nonentified, there is no limit to the entifications it can assume. The Divine Names may be said to be infinite.[12] Thus they must be looked on as the principles and sources of all the individual things existing within the world of manifestation. Here they are no longer called Names and Attributes, but rather "archetypal-entities" (*'ayn*), "realities" (*haqiqah*), and "meanings" (*ma'na*). And when existence is bestowed on them, these very archetypal-entities become the existent-entities of the world. Hence in Arabic and Persian, the one word "entity" (*'ayn*) is used for both the archetypal-entity and the existent-entity, indicating that ultimately the two are one and the same. "Entity" in this sense is synonymous with "thing" (*shay'*) and "quiddity" (*mahiyyah*). All three terms indicate a single reality that may be existent or nonexistent, depending on whether it is considered as manifested within the world or nonmanifest within God's Knowledge (see Figure 2).

In short, by Its very nature Nondelimited Being possesses all possibilities of Self-Manifestation (*zuhur, tajalli*). By Its very nature It is Alive and has Knowledge, Power, Will, Hearing, Sight, Speech. It can assume the entification that is represented by every single "possible existent" (*mumkin*), every creature, every thing. However, that "very nature" is unknowable to us, except through revelation. And even then, the only thing that can be explained is God as He manifests Himself—that is, His Names and Attributes—not God as He is in His very Self. That can only be known by the great prophets and saints within the inmost recesses of their own reality.

When Being is envisaged from the point of view that It embraces all Names, Attributes, and the possible entities, It is called the "First Entification" (*ta'ayyun-i awwal*). At the level of this entification, the infinite possibilities of Self-Manifestation possessed by God are delineated within His Knowledge, but they are all "nonexistent" and nonmanifest.

The First Entification has numerous names, depending on our point of view. Some of these are important for our present discussion

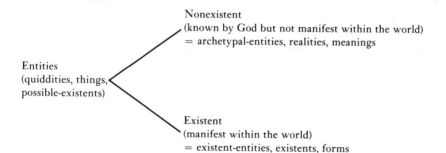

FIGURE 2: PRELIMINARY DIVISION OF THE KINDS OF ENTITIES

INTRODUCTION

1. The First Entification (God's Knowledge of Himself and all things)

2. Oneness
   - Exclusive-Unity (Only God *is*)
   - Inclusive-Unity (God's One Being embraces all Names and Attributes and all entities)

3. The First Isthmus-Nature (The First Entification stands between and comprehends both Nonentification and entification)

4. The Most Holy Effusion = The Unseen Theophany (The First Entification embraces God's Unseen Knowledge of all entities, which become manifest through the Holy Effusion or the Visible Theophany)

5. The Reality of the Perfect Man (The First Entification is the archetypal-entity of the Perfect Man)

FIGURE 3: SOME NAMES OF THE FIRST ENTIFICATION

(see Figure 3): Since the First Entification represents the sum total of all the potentialities of God's Self-Manifestation, but in a state where each potentiality is identical with every other and with Being, it is called "Oneness." Nonentification Itself cannot be referred to as "One," since It is beyond all names and attributes. We can only say, in the manner of the Vedantists, that it is "not this, not that." Qunawi even declares that to call Nonentification "Being" is not strictly correct. "That is not Its true name."[13]

When we observe this Oneness of the First Entification, we see that in respect to its very Self, all many-ness (*kathrah*) is effaced and obliterated. From this point of view it is called "Exclusive-Unity" (*ahadiyyah*), since it *excludes* any kind of multiplicity. If we observe the same Oneness in respect of the infinite ontological potentialities and possibilities of outward manifestation that it embraces, it is called "Inclusive-Unity" (*wahidiyyah*), since, by embracing all the modes of Being, it *includes* the realities of all things.

Since the First Entification is Exclusively-One from one point of view and Inclusively-One from another point of view, it comprehends both Oneness and the Principle of many-ness. Thus it acts as the intermediary between the Essence's Nonentification and the enti-

10

fied creatures, or between the absolute Independence of God and the dependence and need of the existent things. From this point of view it is referred to as the "First Isthmus-Nature" (*barzakhiyyat-i ula*). For an "isthmus" is something that lies between two other things and comprehends the attributes of both.[14] On the one hand the First Entification is One and is nothing other than Being, since it is only different from the Nonentification of the Essence in respect of the fact that it is the potentiality of the Essence's Self-Manifestation. On the other hand, it embraces all the perfections of Being, each of which requires a different locus-of-manifestation, so it is the principle of creation and multiplicity.

As the locus of God's Knowledge of Himself and the station within which "He manifested Himself to Himself in theophany" (*tajalla bi-dhatihi li-dhatihi*), the First Entification comprehends all the archetypal-entities and realities before they enter into outward existence. In this respect it is called the "Most Holy Effusion" (*fayd-i aqdas*) or the "Unseen Theophany" (*tajalli-yi ghaybi*). It is contrasted with the "Holy Effusion" (*fayd-i muqaddas*) or the "Visible Theophany" (*tajalli-yi shahadi*), through which the archetypal-entities act as receptacles for being and become existent-entities, or in other words, through which all the worlds are created. This Holy Effusion is also called the "Second Entification."[15]

In respect of the fact that the First Entification comprehends all the perfections of God and the world in a single, all-comprehensive unity, it is referred to as the "Reality of the Perfect Man," a term that needs to be explained in some detail.[16] For the Perfect Man is not simply a human individual who has reached "perfection." He represents a metaphysical and cosmological principle that embraces the whole of creation and is man's ontological prototype. And here the term "reality" must be understood according to its particular technical significance.

The Perfect Man is central to Ibn al-'Arabi's metaphysics. In a certain sense he corresponds to the Logos, for concerning him we can certainly say that "He was in the beginning with God; all things were made through him, and without him was not anything made that was made" (Jn. 1:2–3). Through the Perfect Man God creates the world, and ultimately this means that the whole of creation is in one sense identical with him. In the Islamic universe the most perfect outward manifestion of the Perfect Man is of course the Prophet Muhammad.

INTRODUCTION

Other prophets and the saints can never quite attain his station. Hence the "Reality of the Perfect Man" is also referred to as the "Muhammadan Reality."

In order to explain the nature of the Perfect Man more thoroughly, we have to refer to the "Five Divine Presences," or, in other words, the five universal planes of Entified Being. These five "ontological levels" (*maratib al-wujud*) or five "worlds" (*'awalim*) summarize all things or entities into five general categories.[17]

In Islamic religious terminology, things are divided into two general kinds: those we are able to see with our physical eyes, and those we cannot see. Thus, in the Koran God is often referred to as the "Knower of the Unseen and the Visible." But as Qunawi explains, there is one entity that is neither totally Visible nor totally Unseen, that is, man and, *a fortiori*, the principle of which man is the manifestation, the Perfect Man. Hence at first sight all of Entified Being can be divided into three kinds. In Qunawi's words, "Although the ontological levels are numerous, they are reducible to the Unseen, the Visible, and the reality which comprehends these two."[18]

As was indicated above, Entified Being can be divided into two basic kinds of entities, the nonexistent and the existent. These two can be said to correspond to the Unseen and the Visible.[19] Nonexistent or Unseen entities are those that are known to God but not manifest within the world. The existent or Visible entities are outwardly manifest within the world. Some of them are completely visible to the naked eye. These things belong to the corporeal world. Others are in close proximity to God, but although "Unseen" in relation to us, they must be considered "Visible" in comparison to God's Unseen Knowledge. These are the Spirits, also referred to as "angels" or "intellects." Finally, some entities stand between the Spirits and the Corporeal-Bodies. These are known as the "Image-Exemplars." They are "luminous" like the Spirits, but unlike them they can appear in corporeal shapes. They form an "isthmus" between the Spirits and Corporeal-Bodies, thus establishing a relationship between the two sides. Without the isthmus the Spirits in their pure luminosity and subtlety would be completely cut off from the Corporeal-Bodies in their unmixed darkness and grossness. These three created worlds—that of the Corporeal-Bodies, the Image-Exemplars, and the Spirits—make up three of the Five Divine Presences. The other two are the uncreated divine Knowledge, and the Perfect Man, who is both created and uncreated at the same time.

INTRODUCTION

When Qunawi enumerates the Five Presences, he usually does so as follows (see Figure 4): The First Presence is the First Entification, or the Presence of Divine Knowledge, also referred to as the "Unseen." The Second Presence, which faces the Unseen in the opposite position, is the World of Corporeal-Bodies or the Visible. This is the "material world," within which man finds himself situated. The Third and Central Presence is that of the Perfect Man, who acts as a partition between the two sides and at the same time comprehends and includes both of them. The Fourth Presence, to the right of the Perfect Man and nearer to the Unseen, is the World of the Spirits or angels, which includes the Universal Intellect (= the Supreme Pen), the first thing created by God. The Fifth Presence, to the left of the Perfect Man and nearer to the Visible, is the World of Image-Exemplars (*mithal*) or Imagination (*khayal*), within which spirits become corporealized and appear to prophets and saints in visions; and within which is the "Isthmus" after death, where moral qualities and works become spiritualized and personified. These five Presences embrace all levels of entification, from the uncreated to the lowest level of the created. Only the Nonentified Essence—Being as such—is outside of them.

Since the Perfect Man encompasses all the Presences, his total macrocosmic nature has five levels: (1) his reality or archetypal-entity, which is the First Entification (here we have the technical usage of the word "reality" in the expression the "Reality of the Perfect Man" referred to above); (2) his spirit, the Universal Intellect, which comprehends the whole of the World of the Spirits and is the first thing created by God; (3) his soul, or the World of Image-Exemplars, which acts as an intermediary between his spirit and his body; (4) his body, which corresponds to the whole of the corporeal world; (5) his nature as such, which comprehends all Presences. Obviously, man as an individual is a "microcosm" reflecting all these levels (Figure 5). And all these levels taken as a whole, which comprise the fifth level—that of the Perfect Man as such—are the mirror image of Nonentified Being.

So all that exists may be divided from a certain point of view into two categories: On the one hand is Nonentified and Nondelimited Being, on the other all the entifications Being assumes, entifications that are comprehended into a Unity by the Perfect Man (see Figure 6).

We have seen that everything other than Nonentified Being is an entity[20] and that the entities are of three kinds: "nonexistent," "exis-

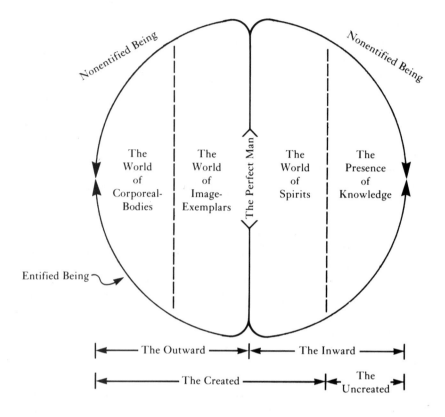

FIGURE 4: THE FIVE DIVINE PRESENCES
(The Perfect Man comprehends all of Entified Being)

tent," and "both nonexistent and existent" (see Figure 7). But here we must follow Qunawi's analysis of Entified Being one step further. We speak of the "existence" of the entities, but, in fact, this is inaccurate. Our starting point was that "Being is One," and that only Being *is*. There are not two or more Beings, two or more existences. The plurality of the entities cannot affect the fundamental axiom of Being's Oneness. So how can we correctly speak of "existents" in the plural? Is it not true that there is only one Existent?

In fact, since Being is One, and since it is the only true Reality, the entities *as entities* have no positive reality. They remain always nonexistent in themselves. Whatever existence they seem to possess is

INTRODUCTION

Individual Man	*The Perfect Man*
1. his archetypal-entity	1. The First Entification
2. his spirit	2. The World of the Spirits
3. his soul	3. The World of Image-Exemplars
4. his body	4. The World of Corporeal-Bodies

FIGURE 5: CORRESPONDENCE BETWEEN INDIVIDUAL MAN
AND THE PERFECT MAN

not their own. It belongs only to God, the only Being there is, the only thing that may truly be said to *exist.*

Being is Light, and nonexistence is darkness. So the nonexistent entities are never themselves outwardly manifested, just as darkness itself is never seen. Whatever is seen is Being, Light, the only reality there is. Only the effects of the nonexistent entities are perceived, in the sense that the removal of certain perfections from Light (= the delimitation of Being) allows us to see colors. But the color, the entity, that which is manifested, is nothing but Light Itself.

So all entities considered in themselves are nonexistent, whereas considered in relation to Being they are the possibilities of Self-Manifestation inherent within It. Hence nothing but Being exists. And Being is One. So when we speak of "existence," we mean Being as delimited, defined, and colored by the entities, or in other words, Be-

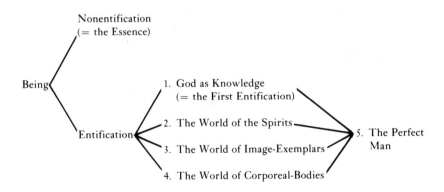

FIGURE 6: THE TOTALITY OF BEING

15

FIGURE 7: COMPREHENSIVE DIVISION OF THE KINDS OF ENTITIES

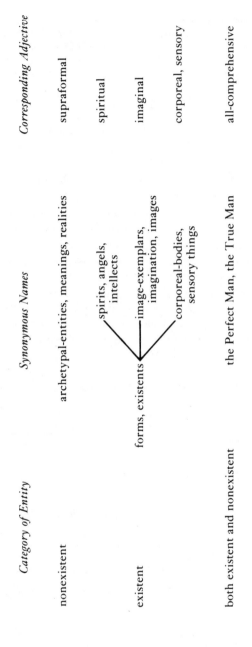

Category of Entity	Synonymous Names	Corresponding Adjective
nonexistent	archetypal-entities, meanings, realities	supraformal
existent	forms, existents — spirits, angels, intellects	spiritual
	image-exemplars, imagination, images	imaginal
	corporeal-bodies, sensory things	corporeal, sensory
both existent and nonexistent	the Perfect Man, the True Man	all-comprehensive

ing as It becomes outwardly manifest in respect to one or more of Its perfections. The Self-Manifestation of Being *as such* is then the Perfect Man, who comprehends all the perfections of Being in their full deployment and in their unity at the same time.

The Perfect Man acts as a receptacle for all of Being's perfections. He does not delimit and define Being, so that some of Its perfections would be visible and others hidden. Hence it is sometimes said that the Perfect Man has no entity.[21] For the "entity" is that which is nonexistent in itself and detracts from Being's pure Radiance. But the Perfect Man reflects Being as such. In this sense he himself is nothing but Sheer Being, and is therefore nonentified.

In short, no matter how much we speak of this and that, things, attributes, colors, entities, delineations, characteristics, properties, these are all nothing but the radiation of Being, nonexistent in themselves. Only the One Being *is*.

Qunawi summarizes the nature of the Oneness of Being in numerous passages, including the following: "God knows all things as a result of His very Knowledge of His own Essence. He is not qualified by any knowledge derived from other than Himself or through other than Himself. Then He bestows being upon the world in accordance with His Knowledge of the world in Himself from Eternity-without-beginning. So the world is the form of and locus-of-manifestation for His Knowledge, and God never ceases to encompass the things in Knowledge and Being.... Everything which becomes manifest becomes manifest only from Him, since nothing else possesses a being which might accompany His Being. This is the news given by the Prophet: 'God is, and nothing is with Him.' "[22]

LOVE: THE MOTIVATING FORCE OF GOD'S SELF-MANIFESTATION

Farghani defines love as "an inward inclination toward reaching a perfection. Its reality is a unifying relation between the seeker and the sought, its meaning is the domination of that which brings about unification and sharing, and its effect is the disappearance of that which brings about differentiation and diversity between the seeker and the sought."[23]

Love, then, begins with consciousness of an imperfection and a desire to eliminate it. The desired perfection becomes the goal or beloved of him who is imperfect, the lover. Moreover, the existence of this inclination depends on a unifying relation between the two sides. This relation is referred to technically as "affinity" (*munasabah*). It is defined as "a property through which unification is brought about between two things."[24] It means that there is already something shared between the lover and the beloved, something on the basis of which the affinity can be said to exist. This something must be strengthened and perfected for the lover to attain his goal, which is the disappearance of those attributes that prevent unification and union. If there were no common factor shared between the two sides, the lover could never make the beloved the object of his quest, for he could never even gain knowledge of the beloved.

Qunawi writes, "It is inconceivable that one thing should love another thing in the respect that that thing differs from it. It can only love that thing as a result of the property of some meaning shared between the two of them, in respect of which an affinity is established between them, an affinity which will lead to the domination of the property of 'that which brings about unification' over the property of 'that which brings about differentiation and separation.' As a result of knowledge and awareness of this affinity, the person who has this knowledge and awareness will seek to remove totally the properties of separation and to manifest the dominating force of 'that which brings about unification.' Then complete union will definitely follow."[25]

Now this love, which depends on an affinity between lover and beloved and which results in union, stems from a Divine prototype. It exists, and like all things that exist, it must derive from the very nature of Being Itself. It must be one of the infinite ontological perfections.

The Divine prototype of love is expressed by means of the words "I loved" (*ahbabtu*) in the famous *hadith qudsi* in which God says, "I was a Hidden Treasure and I *loved* to be known. So I created the creatures that I might be known." The "Hidden Treasure" is an allusion to the infinite ontological perfections of God, which, as we have said, are summarized as the Names and Attributes.

Now the Essence Itself is nonentified. So the level to which the pronoun "I" in "I loved" refers is the First Entification, within which God's Attributes are delimited, defined, and known. For if God is to say "I was a Hidden Treasure," He must have consciousness of this Treasure. Thus God's words refer to the level where we can speak of His Self-Awareness, that is, His Knowledge. Moreover, it is only here that we can speak of the "necessity" for creation, or of a certain imperfection that needed to be overcome, for Being Itself is "Independent of all the worlds" (Koran III:97). In speaking of the "mystery of 'I loved,' " Qunawi remarks that the pronoun "I" refers to the Lord (rabb), since the Lord by His very nature must have a vassal (marbub) over which He can exercise His Lordship.[26] In a similar manner, Ibn al-'Arabi states that each Name and Attribute demands a locus-of-manifestation within which its perfection may be displayed. Hence the Divine Names "demand in themselves the existence of the world."[27]

In order to understand the significance of these remarks by Qunawi and Ibn al-'Arabi, we should recall that love was defined as "an inward inclination toward reaching a perfection." If we say that God possesses Love, are we not maintaining that He is somehow imperfect? The remarks of Ibn al-'Arabi and his disciple mean that God's Love does imply a certain "imperfection" from a certain relative point of view. But this imperfection is in truth a perfection and the source for the appearance of all other perfections.

To review what we have already said, we should recall that a distinction must be made between God as such—the Essence, Nonentified Being—and God as He reveals Himself to us through His Names and Attributes. Being in Its Nonentified Plenitude is perfect in every sense, for It can lack nothing. All things, all perfections, are only Its possibilities of Self-Manifestation actualized. In the words of another of Qunawi's disciples, Being is "that which is *thing* in every respect" (ma huwa ash-shay' min kull wajh).[28] All the infinite things that have existed, do exist, and will exist are nothing but Being's manifestations, precisely because they *exist*. Thus Being possesses all perfections—which are nothing but modes of existence—by Its very nature. To speak of It as "imperfect" is meaningless.

But when we examine Being as entified by the Attributes, that is, at the level where we can say that God possesses such Names as "Living, Knowing, Powerful, Creator, Loving," a certain kind of theoretical imperfection can be envisaged, although it remains purely theoretical and suppositional, since it can never be actualized. Each Name taken as a reality in itself is different from the Essence, although it is nothing but one of the Essence's perfections. But viewed in itself, it can be considered as possessing a certain difference from Being as such. In other words, the "All-Forgiving" (al-ghafur) is nothing but God, but God in His Essence is not identical with the

INTRODUCTION

All-Forgiving in every respect, for He is also the "Vengeful" (*al-muntaqim*).

But Being is One. In the Essence there is no trace of multiplicity. Only at the level of the First Entification can we speak of a potential multiplicity, that is, the Names and Attributes envisaged as separate realities. But here also God is One, each Name is identical in its existence with every other. So in order for the Names and Attributes of God to be anything more than the potentialities of manifestation inherent within Being, in order for each perfection to be viewed in itself as an independent reality, in order for the Hidden Treasure to be displayed, multiplicity must be manifested. As long as there is no creation—as long as the Hidden Treasure remains hidden and the Name "Outwardly-Manifest" (*az-zahir*) remains latent—the properties of God's Names will not be able to show themselves. The Names can have no actualized significance unless there is a world within which each of them can display its properties and characteristics separate from, as well as in combination with, the properties and characteristics of the other Names.

So God's Names would not be displayed if there were no creation. Each would remain identical with every other within the Divine Unity. As a result, God's Names would have no *raison d'être*. For if God is the "Creator," it is so that He can have a creation. If He is "Merciful," it is so that He can exercise His Mercy. Ultimately—in Ibn al-'Arabi's terms—if he is "God" it is so that He can have something to be "god over" (*ma'luh*). So this perfection of the manifestation of His own Attributes is what God seeks to realize through His "Love." The "imperfection" from which He wishes to escape is the nonmanifestation of His own Names and Attributes.

But, of course, there is a great difference between the "imperfection" implied by God's Love and that implied by man's love. God's "imperfection" is only our own mental construct based on the supposition that His Names might not have loci of manifestation within which to display themselves. But they do have such loci, for the universe exists. And since God creates for all eternity—for He is the "Creator" now and forever, His nature never changing—there is no moment or time when He does not possess the perfection that is the object of His Love.

Man and the other creatures, however, are in a constant flux and undergo a perpetual movement toward their respective perfections. The objects of their loves exist separately from them, and they can attain these objects only through temporal becoming. From this point of view we can speak in their case of true imperfection and an inward inclination toward reaching a perfection they do not now possess. It is only when man attains his true and ultimate Beloved, God, that he can elude the process of becoming and find his perfection here and now in the eternal present.

Ibn al-'Arabi and his followers speak about two Perfections God possesses for all eternity. One is the "Essence-derived Perfection" (*al-kamal adh-dhati*), which God possesses in Himself by His very nature as Nondelimited Being. The other is the "Name-derived Perfection" (*al-kamal al-asma'i*), which requires that all the infinite ontological perfections inherent in Nonentified Being become deployed and displayed in outward manifestation.[29]

Qunawi often refers to the object of God's Love, that is, the Name-derived Perfection, as the "Perfection of Distinct-Manifestation and Distinct-Vision" (*kamal al-jala' wa-l-istijla'*).[30] The Perfection of Distinct-Manifestation is actualized when all the ontological perfections inherent within Being (= the Hidden Treasure) receive their full deployment. In other words, this perfection is for the Perfect Man to receive his full outward-manifestation through the deployment of the Divine Presences as a result of the Second Entification.

As for the Perfection of Distinct-Vision, it consists of the knowledge and vision of the Hidden Treasure once it has become deployed. But this knowledge entails several kinds of knowledge at once. First, God's Knowledge of the Hidden Treasure can be none other than His Knowledge of Himself, since God is One. But at the actualization of this perfection, this Knowledge has two dimensions: the Knowledge of the Essence as such, or of the Inward; and the Knowledge of the Hidden Treasure as deployed, or of the Outward. This "Outward" becomes differentiated from God in any true sense only at the level of creation. "Before" creation, it was one with Him in every way. But "after" creation, it can be called "other than God" in respect of its multiplicity and its separation from its source. Moreover, this "other" possesses a certain reality of its own, which includes knowledge and vision. So the Perfection of Distinct-Vision also means that the "other" must contemplate itself in itself inasmuch as it is differentiated from its Source, and likewise it must contemplate God with its own eye and with God's eye as well.

So the other, which knows God both through its own vision and

INTRODUCTION

God's vision, can be no one but the Perfect Man. Only the Perfect Man can know God *as such,* since only he is the mirror for the totality of God's Names and Attributes. In other words, only he has the scope to perceive and thus to know every Attribute of God. All other entities can reflect and perceive only some of God's Names. Or, if certain entities can perceive all of them, they can do so only within a certain ontological level, not within the full range of the deployment of the Names.[31] This is what Ibn al-'Arabi and his followers are referring to when they call the Perfect Man the "all-comprehensive generated-existent" (*al-kawn al-jami'*). The Perfect Man is "generated" since, at least in his external form, he belongs to the world of generation and corruption; or since he is a creature and not the Creator. And he is "all-comprehensive" because he embraces, quite literally, all things, from "God" to the tiniest atom.

It follows from what we have said that only the Perfect Man can truly love God. For love is "an inclination toward reaching a perfection." To truly love God means first of all to know that God *as such* is the perfection one must reach, not God as He reveals Himself through His Names and Attributes. Thus the Perfect Man is called the "servant of Allah," since the master whom he serves and loves is none but the Essence of God, which is named by the All-Comprehensive Name "Allah."[32] No Name and Attribute escapes the Perfect Man's gaze and attentiveness, for he is the mirror of Nondelimited and Nonentified Being. He desires God *as such,* not God as the Merciful, the Generous, the Bountiful. He is the mirror of Being *as such,* not of the various perfections or Attributes that are inherent within Being. Thus Qunawi says, "God cannot be the Sought or the Beloved of anyone, save the Perfect Man."[33]

Man's capacity to love God in a total manner and to become the Perfect Man in whom God contemplates His own Name-derived Perfection is referred to as man's being the "vicegerent" (*khalifah*) of Allah. It is the "trust" about which God says, "We offered the Trust to the heavens and the earth and the mountains, but they refused to carry it and were afraid of it; and man carried it" (Koran XXXIII:72). Farghani writes:

When the First Theophany (= the First Entification) in its totality and in the perfection of its all-comprehensiveness, and in accordance with the property of its holy, Love-derived motion, turned its Attentiveness toward the Perfection

22

of Self-Manifestation and Making-Manifest (i.e., making the entities appear in outward manifestation), only the reality of the First Isthmus-Nature (= the Perfect Man) was its complete vehicle and mirror. . . . God refers to this when He says, "We offered the Trust," i.e., the receptivity for this theophany in its totality, "to the heavens," i.e., the higher things (= the World of the Spirits), "and the earth," i.e., the lower things (= the World of Corporeal-Bodies), "and the mountains," i.e., what is between them (= the World of Image-Exemplars), "but they refused to carry it," because of their need for the perfection of their receptivity in order to bring about the perfection of Outward-Manifestation in a complete manner. They lacked perfect preparednesses and complete correspondence (mudahat) with the reality of that Isthmus-Nature. "They were afraid of it," i.e., they feared to act as a receptacle for it, because they were delimited by the properties of the Names (and not by the property of the All-Comprehensive Name, which manifests Being as such). "And man carried it," because of his perfect receptivity and total correspondence with the reality of that Isthmus-Nature.[34]

Now the reality of love is one of the perfections inherent within Being. And since, according to the Sufi saying, "Being descends with all Its soldiers," love pervades all things. Wherever anything exists, love is there, inherent within the very nature of existence itself. Wherever Being displays Its Radiance, love is busy inciting the existents toward the goal of all, the Perfection of Distinct-Manifestation and Distinct-Vision.

For the goal of creation to be achieved, all of Being's perfections must be deployed within and realized by the Perfect Man. So all the creatures must be actualized within the Divine Presences, since each is a precondition for the actualization of the Perfect Man. Thus each thing is God's beloved, since each thing has its share to play in achieving the desired Perfection. In Qunawi's words, "Whatever is necessary to actualize the Sought is itself the Sought."[35] Whatever is necessary to bring about the total deployment of God's Name-derived Perfection is itself the object of God's Love.

So love pervades all things. All motions and stillnesses, actions and reactions, causes and effects—in short, each thing that exists and

every property and activity it displays—are derived from love. All
have a single goal: to manifest the full scope of their own ontological
possibilities and thus to deploy Being in Its Totality, or, in other
words, to bring about the Perfection of Distinct-Manifestation and
Distinct-Vision.

All derives from love. In Qunawi's words, "When the theophany
of Love pervaded the entities, they sought from God the Outward-
Manifestation of their own realities and perfections. Hence this theophany is the key to all the . . . motions which make the hidden things
manifest and which bring the archetypal-entities . . . out into actuality."[36]

Individual man has a special role to play in bringing about the
Name-derived Perfection. By the fact that he is a man, he manifests
the human reality, which is nothing but the First Entification in respect of the Isthmus-Nature referred to above. But as long as man
does not travel on the Path of spiritual realization, as long as he does
not *actualize* all the potential perfections inherent within himself, he
will not be able to fulfill the role for which he was created. If he does
not reach the station of the Perfect Man, he will have failed to carry
the Trust.

Of course even those human beings who do not attain the station
of perfection still have a role to play, just as all creatures other than
man are necessary for the Name-derived Perfection to be actualized
in its totality. Farghani writes,

God placed man upon the throne of vicegerency and made
him a mirror of the Presence of Divinity and the Form of
the Sanctuary of Lordship.[37] Then He made his elemental
form the primordial ground and the material for all the human forms. Some of these forms are desired in themselves,
like the Perfect Men among the messengers, prophets, and
great saints. And others are desired because of things outside
themselves. Some of the latter are like the causes and precon-
ditions for the entification of the constitution and form of
each Perfect Man, like their fathers and mothers. Others act
as organs and helpers (of the Perfect Men) by populating the
other levels and (spiritual) stations, like the rest of the saints
and the believers. And some are subjected to populating this
world and putting it in order, for Divine Wisdom has de-
creed that the Perfect Men can only reach the station of Per-

fection by means of this world. These last are the commonality of people. This disparity (in the levels of men) is a branch of the disparity that occurred at the primordial ground, when the reality of Love became related to the world and its inhabitants (i.e., at the level of the First Entification and the archetypal-entities).[38]

In short, the beloved of all is the Perfection of Distinct-Manifestation and Distinct-Vision, as a result of which the Perfect Man becomes a mirror embracing the full deployment of every ontological perfection inherent within Being. And the beloved of the Perfect Man is also this perfection, which is nothing but himself. But it is also nothing but Being, for Being is One, and at this station all multiplicity has been reintegrated into Unity. In every case the Beloved is God's perfection, or, rather, God Himself, for His perfection is nothing but His One Being. The Circle has closed upon Itself, Unity has been realized, but now within the framework of the total deployment of Being's perfections in Outward-Manifestation.

God is both Love and the Beloved. And since nothing exists but His One Being, He is also the Lover. But usually by "lover" is meant man the creature, or, in other words, man as God's Self-Manifestation still veiled from himself and before he has realized his potential perfection. Nevertheless, man is also the "beloved," as was indicated above, for only he can become the Perfect Man and thus actualize the ultimate object of God's Love.

Thus Qunawi writes,

The Beloved loves the lover because he is the cause of His Distinct-Vision of His own Perfection within him and the locus within which the dominating-force of His Beauty exercises its influence and spreads its properties. Therefore (man is also) the beloved, (and he) is the mirror of the Lover. Within man God distinctly views His own Beauties, which were latent in His Oneness before the locus-of-theophany (i.e., the Perfect Man) became entified. For (before the manifestation of God's Name-derived Perfection), excessive proximity and selfsameness veiled Him from that (i.e., from this Distinct-Vision). Then, when He gained a Distinct-Vision of Himself in something else—because of the actualization of a kind of distance and differentiation ... —and when He saw His own Beauties in the locus-of-theophany, He loved them with a love which would not have come to Him without the locus and the differentiation referred to, because of the fact that proximity and oneness acted as a veil, as we mentioned.[39]

The object of God's Love is Himself; it is the manifestation of His own Beauties and perfections, known as the "Hidden Treasure." Love then is God, the Lover is God, and the Beloved is God. All are One. Moreover, wherever a lover and beloved appear within creation, they display this oneness. In all cases, love, the lover and the beloved are ultimately one, for Being is One. So a lover loves the manifestation of his own attributes, just as God loves the Perfection of Distinct-Manifestation and Distinct-Vision. Every man is a "transcription of Being" (*nuskhat al-wujud*), so within him all God's Attributes are embraced. For just this reason, he is potentially a Perfect Man. So when man loves something, he loves only himself, that is, his own attributes and ontological perfections as reflected in the beloved. He may love them in God—for God is his very reality, his very Self—or he may love them in the creatures, which also manifest man's own reality, that is, Being as such.

This is why Qunawi writes, "Every lover in reality loves only himself. But the form of the beloved stands before him as a mirror in which he contemplates himself in respect of complete affinity and spiritual parallelism (*muhadhat*). So what is called 'beloved' is a precondition for the lover's love of himself."[40] Love can take place only through the mutual parallelism and affinity that exists between lover and beloved, each of which reflects the other. Ultimately, this is because the prototype of all love—that is, God's love for His Name-derived Perfection—is based on just such a duality.

But the end of love is unity. In the last analysis, God and the Perfect Man are One, for Being is One. We can even say that God as the "Inward" is the Essence or Being as such, whereas God as the "Outward" is the Perfect Man or Being deployed. And God "is the Outward and the Inward" (Koran LVII:3).

DIVINE AND HUMAN LOVE

In discussions of Persian poetry, the question of whether the poetical images employed are only symbols or, on the contrary, represent "real" things is often raised. Is the poet a mystic or a profane

INTRODUCTION

man, or has he perhaps employed two points of view in his poetry?[41]
From our analysis of 'Iraqi's ideas, the reader may have concluded
that as a poet and author 'Iraqi—at least in the *Lama'at*—concerns
himself only with "mystical love."

But this is a premature judgment A careful examination of our
discussion and of the *Lama'at* itself will illustrate the fact that 'Iraqi—
like Qunawi, Farghani, and other members of Ibn al-'Arabi's
school—is not discussing mystical love, nor profane love, nor both together, at least not in any exclusive sense. He is discussing love as
such, in all the forms it may take, whether "mystical love" (man's love
for God), "profane love" (man's love for woman or vice versa), "alle-
gorical love" (*'ishq-i majazi*—love for God as contemplated within His
Self-Manifestation in the form of woman), Divine Love (God's love
for man and the creatures), "creaturely love" (the love of each creature for its own perfection), or any other phenomenon that may be
properly called "love."[42] Each of these is nothing but Nondelimited
Love, which has become entified and delimited in keeping with the
receptacle within which It manifests Itself.

When Ibn al-'Arabi and his followers speak of "Being," they do
not mean the Being of God as opposed to that of the creatures, or vice
versa. They mean Being as such, in all the forms it may take, without
exception. For them the "science of Being" is the science of all sciences, since nothing but Being *is*. If someone can understand this science, he has understood the principle of everything. To grasp the
nature of Being Itself is to grasp the nature of all that exists.

"Love" is one of the primary attributes of Being, which means
that whatever exists must participate in it, just as it must participate
in Being. To understand the nature of Love and its myriad self-manifestations is to grasp the nature of Being Itself, for the two are in fact
one.

Of course one may still want to maintain that 'Iraqi is speaking
basically of a "mystical" concept of love. This is true enough, provided one remembers the close relationship between the words "mysticism" and "mystery." If a mystic is one who has knowledge of the
"mysteries," then certainly 'Iraqi's concept of love is "mystical." In
Ibn al-'Arabi's school the Arabic term that may best be translated as
"mystery" (*sirr*) is practically equivalent to "archetypal-entity." The
mysteries of things are hidden from all but God and the greatest
prophets and saints. Qunawi defines a thing's mystery as its inward
and unseen reality. He says that when we come to understand some-

thing's mystery, we have understood its fundamental nature and those of its inward dimensions that are concealed from its observed and outward existence. "Whoever knows a thing's mystery knows the cause and the peculiarity of that thing. He knows the primordial-ground of its source, the reason for its properties and its outward manifestation, and its hidden and evident concomitants."[43] Moreover, true knowledge of something's mystery means that man must have a direct vision of that thing as it is in itself, that is, a suprarational knowledge that derives from "unveiling."[44]

The teachings of Ibn al-'Arabi's school on Being or on Love pertain to the "mystery" of these realities, and hence we may call these figures "mystics." But in no way does this imply a sentimental or irrational—which is quite different from suprarational—attitude on their part. Nor does it mean they ignore or are unconcerned with the phenomena of this world. In their eyes, love is love, whether it is love for God or love for the human form. God's love for the Perfection of Distinct-Manifestation and Distinct-Vision is the source of all other loves, it is the "mystery" of love. Whoever truly understands it will understand "the reason for love's properties and its outward manifestation (in all the forms it may assume), and its hidden and evident concomitants."

In short, the reader must remember that 'Iraqi's discussion is not limited to love for God or love for the human form. He is analyzing unqualified and nondelimited love, not love of any specific kind. In whatever manner we may be concerned with love, the treatise will be of relevance to us and will serve to turn our attention toward love's very Essence.

NOTES

1. The Sufis of Ibn al-'Arabi's school employ the term "intellect" in two basic senses, which one can usually distinguish in English by the use of capital and small letters. Thus the "Intellect" is the first creation of God, also called the "Holy Spirit" or the "Supreme Pen." It possesses direct knowledge of the realities of all things, which it contemplates in God. Then the "intellect" is the microcosmic reflection of this reality within man, as will become clear below when the Five Divine Presences are discussed. Through different degrees of identification with its own source, man's intellect can come to have direct knowledge of the realities of things as they are known by God. This knowledge is referred to as "unveiling." But to avoid confusion between unveiling and the rational, discursive function of the intellect, the Sufis nor-

INTRODUCTION

mally employ the word "intellect" in a pejorative sense, alluding to the limited powers of man's comprehension as such, cut off from divine illumination. When they do employ the term in a positive sense, they are invariably speaking about the "First Intellect" or the "intellects," i.e., the Spirits or angels. Rumi summarizes their reasons for avoiding the term "intellect" to refer to a positive human function in his verse, "The particular intellect has disgraced the Intellect" (Mathnawi V:463).

All of this helps to explain why in Islam there is no fundamental opposition between "intellect" and "unveiling," or in more Western terms, between "logic" and "mysticism." The Sufis do not deny the findings of the intellect; they only claim that it is inadequate to reach the fundamental truth about things without outside guidance, i.e., first revelation, and then unveiling. They do not deny the teachings of the Peripatetic philosophers in principle; rather, they accept those data for the comprehension of which the unaided intellect is "adequate" (in the Thomist sense). But at the same time they hold that many of the philosophers' teachings are invalid, since they concern matters that transgress the intellect's natural limits. See W. C. Chittick, "Mysticism vs. Philosophy in Earlier Islamic History: The al-Tusi, al-Qunawi Correspondence," *Religious Studies* 17 (1981): pp. 87–104.

2. See the forthcoming book tentatively called *Ascendant Stars of Faith: The Sufism of Sadr al-Din al-Qunawi*, by W. C. Chittick, especially the first treatise translated there, in which Qunawi presents the Sufi point of view concerning these matters.

3. See W. C. Chittick, "The Last Will and Testament of Ibn al-'Arabi's Foremost Disciple and Some Notes on Its Author," *Sophia Perennis*, IV, no. 1 (Spring 1978): 43–58; also *Ascendant Stars*, chap. 3.

4. A translation and analysis of Ghazzali's work is being prepared by Nasrollah Pourjavady. Part of what is said here about the relationship between 'Iraqi and Ghazzali is based on discussions with Pourjavady.

5. See the chapter "Knowledge and Love" in T. Burckhardt, *An Introduction to Sufi Doctrine* (Lahore, 1950).

6. Qunawi, *Tabsirat al-mubtadi wa tadhkirat al-muntahi*, part I, 1; translated in *Ascendant Stars*.

7. See W. C. Chittick, "Sadr al-Din Qunawi on the Oneness of Being," *International Philosophical Quarterly* 21 (1981): pp. 171–184.

8. In order that the present discussion be kept within bounds, certain statements will be made that would obviously need much more clarification were a complete philosophical exposition of the subject at hand being attempted. But that is hardly the purpose of the present work. The whole of the enormously fruitful philosophical tradition of Islam, especially after Ibn al-'Arabi, concerns itself largely with clarifying the nature of Being. Such figures as Ibn Turkah Isfahani, Mulla Sadra, Sabziwari, and dozens of others concerned themselves primarily with delimiting and defining this most non-delimited and undefinable of all realities.

INTRODUCTION

One of the most important discussions with which many of these figures occupied themselves was proving that Being is not a mental construct, but is rather "principial" (*asil*). It is concretely existent in Itself in the most real of all senses and is the source of all that exists. Jami devotes part of the introduction of his commentary on the present work to proving that "Being" is not an abstract term. On the importance of the discussion of Being in Islamic philosophy, see T. Izutsu, *The Concept and Reality of Existence* (Tokyo, 1971); and H. Corbin, *Le livre des pénétrations métaphysiques* (Téhéran-Paris, 1964).

9. See the commentary on Flashes VII, X and XXIV.

10. One should qualify this statement by recalling that there are also "impossible things," i.e., imaginary things that because of the very nature of Being cannot exist outside of the mind.

11. Jami, *Naqd an-nusus*, ed. W. C. Chittick (Tehran, 1977), pp. 26, 84.

12. See *Ascendant Stars*, Glossary: NAME.

13. *An-Nusus*, appended to Kashani's *Sharh manazil as-sa'irin* (Tehran, 1315/1897–1898), p. 296; also appended to Ibn Turkah's *Tamhid al-qawa'id* (Tehran, 1316/1898–1899), p. 212; the same passage also occurs in Qunawi's *Miftah al-ghayb*, on the margin of al-Fanari's *Misbah al-ins* (Tehran, 1323/1905–1906), p. 79.

14. See *Ascendant Stars:* ISTHMUS.

15. The whole discussion of the First and Second Entifications, the various names by which each may be called, and the distinction between the two in the views of different Sufis is exceedingly complex. In the above paragraphs we have largely followed Jami's introduction to his commentary on the *Lama'at*, which itself is based primarily upon the views of Sa'iduddin Farghani, whose writings are based explicitly on Qunawi's lectures. Qunawi himself does not discuss these points systematically in his works, but he does allude to them. His most explicit discussion is found in *Tahrir al-bayan fi taqrir shu'ab al-iman* and *al-Hadiyah* (see *Ascendant Stars*). Other members of Ibn al-'Arabi's school often treat the various levels of entification differently. In particular, it is common for them to identify the First and Second Entifications with the levels of *ahadiyyah* and *wahidiyyah* respectively.

16. For further discussion of the Perfect Man, although not completely within the context of Qunawi's teachings, see W. C. Chittick, "The Perfect Man as the Prototype of the Self in the Sufism of Jami," *Studia Islamica* 49, (1979): 135–157.

17. For a much more thorough development of this concept and the different forms it takes, see W. C. Chittick, "The Five Divine Presences: From al-Qunawi to al-Qaysari," *Studia Islamica*, forthcoming.

18. *I'jaz al-bayan fi tafsir umm al-Qur'an* (Hyderabad-Deccan, 1368/1949), p. 113; also as *at-Tafsir as-sufi li-l-Qur'an*, ed. A. A. 'Ata' (Cairo, 1389/1969), p. 221.

19. Depending on the point of view and the context, the term "Unseen" may be wider in scope, in which case its correlative "Visible" will be narrow-

er. The same sort of relationship holds true for many correlative terms. See the commentary on Flash VIII.

20. The term "entity" is the most common expression in Ibn al-'Arabi's school for what is called a "quiddity" (*mahiyyah*) by most of the Moslem philosophers. Practically all of Islamic philosophy—especially the later schools—devotes a good deal of attention to the question of the distinction between being (or existence) and quiddity.

21. See the commentary on Flashes X and XXI. Qunawi refers to this station as the "Point at the Center of the Circle" (*nuqtah wasat ad-da'irah*). See *Ascendant Stars:* CIRCLE.

22. *I'jaz al-bayan*, p. 112/220. On the translation of the *hadith* employing "is" instead of "was," see Ibn al-'Arabi's remarks quoted by Jami, *Naqd an-nusus*, p. 93, note 96.

23. *Mashariq ad-darari*, ed. S. J. Ashtiyani (Mashhad, 1357/1978), p. 606.

24. Qunawi, *an-Nafahat al-ilahiyyah* (Tehran, 1316/1898–1899), p. 220.

25. Ibid., pp. 64–65.

26. *Miftah al-ghayb*, p. 150.

27. W. C. Chittick, "Ibn al-'Arabi's own Summary of the Fusus: 'The Imprint of the Bezels of Wisdom,' " *Sophia Perennis* 1, no. 2 (Autumn 1975): 88–128; 2, no. 1 (Spring 1976): 67–106 (1, no. 2, p. 94).

28. 'Afifuddin at-Tilimsani, *Sharh al-fusus*, "al-fass al-ibrahimi," Ms. Şehid Ali Paşa 1248 (Süleymaniye Library, Istanbul).

29. See Qunawi, *an-Nusus*, p. 287/199; also Farghani, *Mashariq ad-darari*, p. 17.

30. See *I'jaz al-bayan*, pp. 118/226–128/236, where Qunawi describes in detail the whole process of creation and its relation to Love in terms of this perfection.

31. Each of the Presences reflects all of God's Names and Attributes, but in a limited manner, since it can reflect them only at its own ontological level. Thus, for example, the Universal Intellect—also called the "Supreme Pen" and identified with the archangel Gabriel—embraces all that exists, but only at the level of the Spiritual World. Things that become manifest in ontological levels below it are embraced by it only in principle. It always remains transcendent in relation to the World of Image-Exemplars and the World of Corporeal-Bodies, since its level is that of Intellect and Spirit. It may become manifest in the lower worlds, but in itself it does not enter into them.

32. On the importance of this Name in this respect, see Chittick, "The Perfect Man."

33. *Miftah al-ghayb*, p. 256.

34. *Mashariq ad-darari*, p. 57. See *Ascendant Stars:* TRUST; also, "The Perfect Man."

35. *Al-Fukuk*, on the margin of Kashani's *Sharh manazil as-sa'irin* (Tehran, 1315/1897–1898), p. 227.

36. *I'jaz al-bayan*, pp. 122/230–123/231.

37. The reader should remember the famous *hadith:* "God created Adam upon his own Form." See "The Perfect Man."

38. *Mashariq ad-darari,* p. 52.

39. *An-Nafahat al-ilahiyyah,* p. 60.

40. *I'jaz al-bayan,* p. 210/324.

41. See A. Schimmel, *Mystical Dimensions of Islam* (Chapel Hill, N.C., 1975), pp. 288ff.

42. Jami classifies the different kinds of love in his *Lawami'.*

43. *I'jaz al-bayan,* p. 245/359–360.

44. See Flash VIII; also *Ascendant Stars:* UNVEILING.

II   The Life of 'Iraqi[1]

Fakhruddin Ibrahim, called 'Iraqi,[2] was born in the village of Kamajan near the city of Hamadan about 610/1213. His ancestors had been men of knowledge and culture. A month before his birth, his father dreamed of 'Ali ibn Abi Talib (the son-in-law of the Prophet Muhammad, fourth caliph of Sunni Islam and the first imam of Shi'ite Islam, and after the Prophet the model *par excellence* for all Sufis). 'Ali stood with a gathering of saints in a garden. Someone came forward and placed a child on the ground in front of 'Ali, who picked it up; then, calling the father to him, 'Ali gave the child to him and said, "Take our 'Iraqi and raise him well, for he will be a world-conqueror!" The father woke from his sleep with joy. "When 'Iraqi was born", he related, "I looked at his face and realized that he appeared to be the very child of my dream."

At the age of five, the boy was sent to school. In nine months he had memorized the entire Koran, and in the evenings he would recite in a sweet voice the portion that had been his task that day, sometimes weeping, until all who heard his melodious voice grew sad and restless. The neighbors were fascinated by him, and could hardly wait each evening for his recitation. A group of children, too, had lost their hearts to him, and he to them. He could not rest quiet one moment without them. Each day when they were free from school, they would run off after 'Iraqi. By the time he was eight he was famous throughout Hamadan. Every day after the afternoon prayer he would recite from the Koran, and great numbers of people would gather to listen.

One day at the mosque he happened to be reciting the Surah Taha, his portion for the day. A number of non-Muslims were passing by just at the moment he reached the verse, "And so do We reward the prodigal, who believeth not in the signs of his Lord. Surely,

INTRODUCTION

the punishment of the world to come is more severe and enduring"
(XX:127). Three of them suddenly stopped to listen, then were drawn
into the mosque, and finally fell at 'Iraqi's feet and joyfully accepted
Islam at his hands. The entire population of the city assembled, pa-
raded the converts with great honor through the streets, and offered
them money. They refused to accept even a penny, however, but returned home and expounded the faith to their relatives and children,
five of whom were likewise converted.

By the age of seventeen 'Iraqi had learned all the sciences, both
the "transmitted" and the "intellectual," and had already begun to
teach others.[3]

One day it happened that a company of wandering dervishes or
"Kalandars" came to the city.[4] They began to hold one of their meet-
ings, and with sweet melody to chant the following verses:

> We've moved our bedrolls from the mosque to the
>   tavern of ruin;
> we've scribbled over the page of asceticism and
>   erased all miracles of piety.
> Now we sit in the ranks of lovers in the
>   Magi's lane
> and drink a cup from the hands of the
>   dissolute haunters of the tavern.
> If the heart should beat the drum of
>   respectability now, why not?
> For we've raised the flag of our fortune
>   to high heaven.
> We've passed beyond all self-denial, all
>   mystical "stations";
> after all, have we not drained from all those states
>   the cup of hardship?

'Iraqi beheld this wild crew, and the flame of love caught at the haystack of his reason and consumed it. He tore off his turban and robe
(the dress of the theological student) and gave them to the Kalandars,
saying:

> How if my bosom friend, my beloved,
> my intimate, how sweet, if it were you.

34

INTRODUCTION

If you compounded a medicine for my heart,
    racked with pain, if you cured my soul, how sweet.
I would swell so with joy the earth could not hold me
if for just one moment you would drink my grief.
    My affairs are difficult, but how simple
    this business would be, if you'd mix yourself in it.
Let the whole world declare war on me,
what would I fear, with you to defend me?
    Like a dawn nightingale I weep and weep at a perfume
    which hints that you might become my rose.
Should I ever describe the beauty of a face like a moon
or refer to cheeks traced with tresses, I'll write of you
    and whether I mention your name or not
    you'll be the target of all my words.
    I—'Iraqi—am binding my heart to you
    for I want you, you, as my beloved.

After some time, the Kalandars left Hamadan and set out for Is-
fahan. No sooner had they vanished than 'Iraqi was overcome with
longing for them. He began by throwing away all his books:

From all of the *Great Remembrances* he gleaned only
    forgetfulness!
As for grammar, he declared it yammer!
Avicenna's *Allusions* he branded delusions!
The Signs of Exoteric Revelation became *The Mysteries of Esoteric
    Interpretation!*
As for the *Container of All*, he emptied it!
As for *The Compendium of Details*—he overlooked them!
As for *The Garden of Astronomers*, the only fruit he plucked
    therein was *The Games of Lovers!*[5]

And the tongue of rational discourse he transmuted to the language of spiritual ecstasy. In short, like one already detached from the
world, he set off in pursuit of those wanderers, and had walked two
miles when he caught up with them. Whereupon he recited:

I have seen that the lane of piety stretches out,
    far, far into the distance;

INTRODUCTION

My dearest friends, can you not show me then
    the way of the madman?
Bring me a glass of Magian wine
    that I may drink deep
for I have given up all thought
    of ascetic piety;
or if the pure wine has all been downed
    bring me the cloudy dregs
for thick residue lights up the heart
    and illuminates the eyes.
Tuppence for the Sufi meeting house!
    I flee the company of the righteous;
fill up a row of glasses with wine
    and bring me the first.
I have no rules or regulations,
    nor heart nor religion—
only I remain, and you, sitting in the corner,
    and the wealth of Poverty.
All fear of God, all self-denial I deny;
    bring wine, nothing but wine
for in all sincerity I repent
    my worship which is but hypocrisy.
Yes, bring me wine, for I have
    renounced all renunciation
and all my vaunted self-righteousness
    seems to me but swagger and self-display.
Now for a time let my proof be wine
    against the sorrow of Time
for only in drunkenness can one be free
    of the hour's grief.
Once I am thoroughly drunk, what difference
    if I end up in a church or in Mecca?
Once I've abandoned myself, what matter
    if I win Union—or separation?
I've been to the gambling house and seen
    that the losers there are pure;
I've been to the monastery and have found
    no one but hypocrites.
Now I've broken my repentance, at least
    do not break our covenant:

at least welcome this broken heart and say
    "How are you? Where have you been?"
I've been to Mecca, to circle the Kaaba
    but they refused me entrance
saying "Off with you! What merit have you earned
    outside, that we should admit you within?"
Then, last night, I knocked
    at the tavern door;
from within came a voice: " 'Iraqi! Come in!
    for you are one of the chosen!"

The Kalandars received him with great joy. At once they sat him down, shaved his hair and eyebrows (an offense against pious custom) and, in short, made him one color with themselves. He continued with them on their wanderings through Persia, and eventually to India.

In Multan (in what is now Pakistan) they stopped for a time at the hospice of Shaykh Baha'uddin Zakariyya' Multani. He was the head of the Suhrawardi Order, and the direct successor of Shihabuddin Suhrawardi of Baghdad (539/1145–632/1234; the second great Suhrawardi master). Baha'uddin was born in 578/1182 in Multan, descendant of the Meccan tribe, the Quraysh, to which the Prophet belonged. He was already a man of great spiritual attainment when, while returning overland from a pilgrimage to Mecca, he met Shihabuddin Suhrawardi in Baghdad and was initiated by him. After a period of following the discipline of the Suhrawardiyyah Order, Baha'uddin received in a dream a mantle or cloak from the Throne of God, and on waking from sleep, actually found it on himself. In most cases, Sufi masters receive such cloaks from their own masters as a mark of their spiritual rank when they are appointed as their successors. But according to this account, Baha'uddin's station was so exalted that his mandate to be a master derived directly from God without any intermediary. Of course the account goes on to say that in the same night, he was also appointed as a master by Suhrawardi, who gave him two more cloaks, one handed down from the Prophet himself, and the other Suhrawardi's own. In an ecstatic vision Baha'uddin received from God the titles of *Qutb* (Pole of the Age), *Ghawth* (Support of Islam), and even two names usually reserved for God Himself: *Kabir* (the Great) and *Munir* (the Enlightener).

When Baha'uddin returned to Multan, the Suhrawardiyyah Order had already been introduced to India, but under his leadership it took root and spread. He was extremely wealthy, and kept court like a nobleman; this was in contrast to the more austere style of other Indian orders, such as the Chishtiyyah. No one ever criticized Baha'uddin himself for this elegance, for his greatness and spiritual rank were undisputed; but it is true that the Suhrawardiyyah never gained a wide following among the populace and today is very small.[6]

'Iraqi and his companions were given hospitality by Shaykh Baha'uddin, and had the honor of kissing his hand. The saint, looking over the crew of Kalandars, at once fastened his gaze on 'Iraqi as if he seemed to recognize the youth. "That young man has complete and total 'preparedness,'" he remarked to his close disciple, 'Imaduddin. "He should remain with us." 'Iraqi himself felt a great attraction for the saint, but did not want to stay; he urged his companions to leave as quickly as possible, saying, "Just as a magnet draws iron, so the Shaykh will capture me. We must go at once!"

So they departed, and came to Delhi, where they stayed awhile. After a time they grew bored with Delhi and decided to leave for Somnath. But on the sixth day of their journey a great storm blew up, and 'Iraqi with one other companion became separated from the rest. In longing for his friends, 'Iraqi wept copiously and recited:

> Where is the intimate of my soul
>   who drinks my grief?
> Where is that desire
>   of all the world?
> that soul of the world? that Witness
>   of the spirit of men and djinn?
> Ah! bewildered and mad with love am I:
>   where is that sweet friend?

After wandering for a day and a night they found themselves in the morning back at the gates of Delhi. They waited for some days in the city, but when no news of their companions reached them, 'Iraqi resolved to return to Shaykh Baha'uddin, and spoke with his companion about his intention. The Kalandar however refused to accompany him, saying that he preferred to remain in Delhi.

When 'Iraqi arrived back at the hospice in Multan, the saint received him, but chided him: "'Iraqi, you fled from us!" 'Iraqi replied:

INTRODUCTION

My heart will not
    for an instant
        flee from you
for how can the body
    wrench itself
        from the soul?
The nursemaid
    of your kindness
        folded me in its arms;
Even before my mother
    it fed me with
        a hundred kinds of milk.

At once the Shaykh directed him to make a forty-day retreat, and set
him in a cell. For ten days he sat, and saw no one. But on the eleventh
day, overcome by ecstasy, he wept aloud and sang:

First wine that filled the cup
    they borrowed from the saki's drunken eyes
and finding themselves still among revellers
    poured out the bowl of selflessness.
What fell from the grail—
    her redstained lips—they called "lovers' wine."
And of her dark curls made a net
    for the hunt of the hearts of the world.
They pounded and mixed the pain
    of the universe and called it "love".
The tips of idols' tresses never ceased to stir—
    so much did they agitate the lovers' hearts.
For drunkards' candies they gather
    pista from lips, almonds from eyes;
from that mouth so to be praised
    the love-sick garner but abuse.
This hall has room for good and bad
    one cup for vulgar and Elect alike;
these glances speak epics to the soul
    these eyebrows signal gospel to the heart.
Lovelocks set a trap
    each breath finds its prey . . .

INTRODUCTION

Behind the screen discussing secrets
then openly revealing all—
They are so free with their treasures—
why then should they blame 'Iraqi?

Some of the other dervishes happened to overhear him, and at once ran and told the master what was going on. The Suhrawardi rule was strict, and limited its adherents to ordinary pious activities. Certain dervishes were already suspicious of the wild Kalandar youth, and this new outrage upset them even more. But the master, after listening to their complaints, told them, "Such behavior may be prohibited to *you*—but not to him!"

A few days later, the chief disciple, 'Imaduddin, was passing through the bazaar when he heard 'Iraqi's poem being chanted to the accompaniment of music, which is frowned on by many of those who uphold the letter of the religious law.[7] Passing by the forbidden taverns, he found the same thing: Somehow the poem had "escaped" from 'Iraqi's retreat, and become a hit in the less respectable quarters of the city. He returned to the master and reported what he had heard, and recited the last line of the poem. "His business is finished!" exclaimed the master; and he immediately got up and strode to the door of 'Iraqi's cell.

" 'Iraqi!" he called. "Do you say your prayers in taverns? Come out!" The poet emerged from his cell, and weeping laid his head at the master's feet. But Shaykh Baha'uddin raised 'Iraqi's head from the dust, and would not let him return to his cell. The youth recited:

In the street of wineshops, when
    should I pray? since my
drunkenness and sobriety alike
    are all the same as prayer.
There, no one accepts the coin
    of righteousness, piety and self-denial:
The only good currency in that street
    is beggary.
None but the drunkard knows
    the tavern's secrets—
how could the sober unveil
    the mysteries of that street?

INTRODUCTION

As soon as I met those
     cunning haunters of the wineshop
I realized that other work than theirs
     is nothing but a fable.
Do you want a guided tour
     of the Mecca of Love?
Come, sit in the tavern, for the trip
     to Arabia is long and tedious.
They refused me entrance at first
     at the wineshop
so I went to the monastery
     and found an open door—but
I heard a voice from within the tavern
     crying, " 'Iraqi!
Open the door for yourself, for the gates
     of drunkenness are always agape!"

At once the Shaykh took off his cloak and dressed 'Iraqi in it. He also betrothed his own daughter to him, and the marriage was celebrated the same evening. Of this union a son was born, named Kabiruddin.

'Iraqi remained in Multan in the service of Baha'uddin for twenty-five years. During this time he continued to compose poetry, and his reputation grew—and survives to this day in the whole Persian-speaking world, including India. He was never very prolific, and his entire collected works can be contained in a single average-sized volume.[8] Aside from his shorter works, which consist mostly of brief lyrics and quatrains, he wrote a longer anecdotal poem called the 'Ushshaq-namah,[9] which he dedicated to Shamsuddin Juwayni the vizier, whom he met in Turkey near the end of his life, as we shall see. But his great masterpiece is the present work, the Lama'at, which he also composed later in Turkey. Long philosophical treatises or extended narratives were not his forte, and he is loved precisely for his light touch, his musicality, his daring and even shocking imagery, and his ability to express the most profound Sufi teachings in a vivid and simple style.

At last, Shaykh Baha'uddin felt his death approaching. He sent for 'Iraqi and appointed him his successor in the Order; he then (in 666/1267–1268) passed over to the divine mercy. His magnificent tomb can still be visited in Multan today.

INTRODUCTION

When the other dervishes realized that 'Iraqi had been set over them, they were inflamed with jealousy and hatred. Among themselves they plotted, and chose messengers to present their accusations to the sultan.[10] "This 'Iraqi," the messengers said, "whom the saint has been misled into choosing as his successor, does not preserve the rule, but spends his time reciting poetry in the company of young boys."

The sultan, who had long hated and feared the power of the Order, seized this opportunity to wreak vengeance and assert his control. He sent a messenger with an order for 'Iraqi to appear at court, but the poet at once decided to leave Multan. He said his farewells to the dervishes; heedless of those who sought his life, a few of his friends, men of purity and faith, determined to accompany his flight. So the band set out to the coast, where they embarked by sea, intending to go to Mecca.[11]

They arrived in Oman, and news of their approach reached the ears of the sultan of that country—for 'Iraqi's reputation had preceded him. The sultan happily prepared to receive the travelers, and with a company of nobles went out to meet them. When they arrived the sultan served them drinks with his own hand, set 'Iraqi on his own horse, and led the companions with honor and respect to the city. There the sultan lodged them in his own hospice, where they were well looked after. 'Iraqi was appointed chief shaykh of the district, and was waited on by all the local divines, Sufis, and men of piety, who came—as it were—to test their own currency against the touchstone of his presence.

Time went by, and the travelers had recovered from the fatigue of their journey; and since the season of the Pilgrimage to Mecca was now approaching, they begged the sultan for permission to depart. They saw that he was unwilling to let them go, so, putting their trust in God, they set forth in secret. The sultan heard of this, and attempted to follow them; but as he mounted his horse the beast stumbled and threw him. So he stayed; but sent some of his officials after 'Iraqi's party with gifts of cash. The sultan ordered them to explain his desires to 'Iraqi and try to persuade him to return. If he agreed, good. If not, then (he told them) they must give these poor gifts to the poet's servants, to provide for the journey. But while the messengers went one way, 'Iraqi and his party went another.

Wherever they went, they were received with honor. At last they joined the caravan to Mecca, donned the Pilgrim's robes and per-

INTRODUCTION

formed the Rites. While in Mecca and Medina (where he spent three nights at the Prophet's tomb), 'Iraqi composed several odes, one on Divine Unity, and one in praise of Mohammed. Finally they bade farewell to the sacred lands—though three of the party decided to remain there—and joined a Syrian caravan setting out for Damascus.

From Damascus 'Iraqi and two companions traveled north into Turkey (called "Rum," or Rome, because it had been the seat of the Byzantine Empire), and eventually landed in Konya. Here he had the chance to meet two of the most outstanding Sufis of his own time, and indeed of all times: Sadruddin Qunawi (d. 673/1274) and Mawlana Jalaluddin Rumi (d. 672/1273). 'Iraqi was on good terms with Rumi—in fact, some of Rumi's disciples were later to number 'Iraqi among Rumi's devotees. He often attended Rumi's sessions of music, poetry, and dancing (which undoubtedly influenced his own spiritual and creative work); and he is known to have attended Rumi's funeral ceremonies. After moving to Tokat, 'Iraqi would often speak of Rumi; he would sigh and say, "No one ever understood him as he should have been understood. He came into the world a stranger, and left it a stranger".[12] But with Qunawi he established a much closer relationship: for 'Iraqi, Qunawi was to become a second master, who shaped him intellectually as much as Baha'uddin had shaped him spiritually.

Sadruddin Qunawi was the son of a famous and outstanding Sufi shaykh of Konya named Majduddin, known as "The Teacher of Sultans" because of his friendship with the ruler of the city. Majduddin was a companion and admirer of the great Andalusian shaykh Muhyi'uddin ibn al-'Arabi. When Majduddin died, his widow (Qunawi's mother) married Ibn al-'Arabi, who came to consider the youth as his own son. Ibn al-'Arabi bestowed on Qunawi his full spiritual attention, and eventually named him his Khalifah or chosen successor.[13]

Qunawi was simultaneously the disciple of another of Ibn al-'Arabi's favorite companions, the Suhrawardi shaykh Awhaduddin Kirmani (d. 635/1238),[14] who also treated Qunawi as a close disciple. Qunawi's association with Kirmani lasted some fifteen or sixteen years. Qunawi always used to say, "I have drunk milk from the breasts of two mothers"—meaning Ibn al-'Arabi and Kirmani—and in his last will and testament he asked to be buried in the robe of Ibn al-'Arabi and laid out on the prayer carpet of Kirmani. The mingled influence of these two shaykhs in Qunawi would have appealed to 'Iraqi; for while Ibn al-'Arabi was a unique combination of ecstatic visionary and profound "theosopher," Kirmani was a poet and lover in 'Iraqi's own special style.

Furthermore, 'Iraqi would have felt at home in Qunawi's presence. Undoubtedly the fact that Qunawi had a Suhrawardi initiation must have appealed to him. Moreover, Qunawi was in many ways very like Shaykh Baha'uddin Zakariyya' Multani: both a Sufi and a master of religious law and traditions. In fact, Qunawi was the chief shaykh of Konya, and his household was rather aristocratic.

All this was very much the opposite of Rumi's style of Sufism; in fact, Rumi loved to poke fun at religious scholars and theologians, and lived a very simple and humble life, holding no official positions. At first there had been a certain coolness between Qunawi and Rumi, but when they finally met, all their differences vanished and they became close friends. A number of anecdotes attest to this friendship.

Once, for example, a famous shaykh visited Konya, and met both Rumi and Qunawi. When it came time for the evening prayer, the two insisted that the distinguished visitor lead it. Now, in leading the prayer, one may choose any chapter of the Koran one likes to recite in each of two portions of the prayer. Usually one chooses two different chapters, although it is not incorrect to repeat the same chapter twice. In the first portion, the visiting shaykh recited the chapter, "Say: 'O unbelievers, I worship not what you worship. . . . To you your religion, and to me my religion!' " (CIX). Then, in the second portion, he recited the same chapter again. When the prayer was finished, Rumi turned to Qunawi and remarked dryly, "It seems he recited it once for you, and once for me!" When Rumi died, Qunawi was asked to lead the prayers at his funeral, but he survived him by only a few months.

Among the other students of Qunawi who might well have been with him when 'Iraqi arrived, one should mention Sa'iduddin Farghani, 'Afifuddin at-Tilimsani from North Africa, and Mu'ayyiduddin Jandi. Farghani is the author of a lengthy commentary on one of the most famous Arabic Sufi poems on "love and wine," the *Nazm as-suluk* or "Poem of the Way" of Ibn al-Farid.[15] Farghani wrote this work first in Persian, basing it on lectures delivered by Qunawi, and then translated it himself into Arabic. The Arabic version became one of the most influential works on metaphysics in Ibn al-'Arabi's school. Farghani is also the author of a Persian work on the Shari'ah and the fundamental importance of its practice for Sufis, entitled *Minhaj al-'ibad*. Jandi is the author of one of the longest, earliest, and most widely read commentaries on Ibn al-'Arabi's masterpiece, *Fusus al-hikam.*[16] His Persian *Nafthat ar-ruh wa tuhfat al-futuh* is a summary in two parts of Sufi doctrine and practice. Finally at-Tilimsani was originally Ibn al-'Arabi's disciple, but even before Ibn al-'Arabi's death he became Qunawi's closest companion. He is the author of important Arabic commentaries on *Fusus al-hikam* and an-Niffari's *al-Mawaqif,*[17] as well as a *Diwan* of Arabic poetry. Qunawi left his own works to him when he died.[18]

Unlike 'Iraqi, Qunawi was a retiring man who led an outwardly uneventful life, devoted to writing and teaching; and it is largely through his brilliant books and his equally brilliant and philosophically minded students that he achieved his task, as Ibn al-'Arabi's foremost disciple, of passing on and adding to the Andalusian mystic's teachings. At first it might seem that this man would make an odd teacher for 'Iraqi, the "drunken" poet and former Kalandar, who was, moreover, already a middle-aged and respected shaykh in his own right. But at the time 'Iraqi arrived in Konya, Qunawi was giving a series of lectures on Ibn al-'Arabi's most difficult and important text, *Fusus al-hikam,* and 'Iraqi was able to join the master's other students. 'Iraqi's biographer says that he derived great benefit from this instruction, as well as from a study of Ibn al-'Arabi's *Meccan Revelations (Al-Futuhat al-Makkiyyah).* Qunawi, for his part, conceived a great affection for 'Iraqi, and came to regard him more and more highly as time passed.

Each day, after leaving Qunawi's lecture on the *Fusus,* 'Iraqi would compose a short meditation in mixed prose and verse. Finally he collected them, and called them *Lama'at* or "flashes" of light. His model for this style of composition, as he himself stated, was the famous *Sawanih* of Ahmad Ghazzali (brother of the better-known Sufi author Abu Hamid Ghazzali). Ahmad Ghazzali (d. 520/1126) was, like 'Iraqi, a Sufi of the "School of Love"; both of them were initiating shaykhs, both of them were masters of the Persian language. So it is not surprising that 'Iraqi admired Ghazzali enough to imitate him. The *Sawanih* consists of a number of loosely connected meditations on the themes of Love, Beauty, the lover and Beloved, interspersed with poems and anecdotes, written in a highly dense but clear and elegant manner. In adopting this style, 'Iraqi developed his own philosophy of Love; he borrowed some of Ghazzali's terminology and some of Ibn al-'Arabi's (as expounded by Qunawi), but the overall conception, and the synthesis, were his own. Through this work, more per-

INTRODUCTION

haps than any other, the theosophy of Ibn al-'Arabi was recreated and integrated into the Persian poetic tradition, and its influence on later poets cannot be overestimated.[19]

When 'Iraqi had finished his work, which, like the *Fusus*, consists of twenty-eight chapters, he submitted it to Qunawi for approval. Shaykh Sadruddin read it; then, kissing the volume and pressing it against his eyes (as one does with a sacred book), he exclaimed, " 'Iraqi, you have published the secret of men's words. The *Lama'at* is in truth the pith of the *Fusus!*"

'Iraqi remained a great devotee of Qunawi. Some years later, during a protracted trip to Medina, 'Iraqi wrote to him complaining of their separation and excusing his own absence from Konya. The previously undiscovered letter is worth quoting in its entirety. Besides giving some idea of 'Iraqi's high regard for his teacher, it represents his only known prose work other than the *Lama'at*.[20]

'IRAQI'S LETTER TO QUNAWI

Praise belongs to God, and peace be upon His chosen servants.

In the heart of your sincere servant 'Iraqi, love—which incites unrest and is mixed with pain, and which constantly rattles the chain of desire and strife and ignites the flame of longing and rapture—has kindled the flame of my passion and burnt the haystack of my life's course to such an extent that its fire can be snuffed out only with the earth of the lane, and the muddied course of my life can be purified only with the water of the visage of our lord, the Manifest Guide and Great Conjunction, the Leader (*sadr*) of the Shari'ah and the Tariqah, the Locus-of-Theophany for God and the Truth—may he remain forever a refuge for the people of the Way and an authority for the masters of Verification.

> Where is that loved one? For even though I have reached your door, I am still troubled.
> Where will I find that luck? that you will come sweetly through my door.

From the intensity of separation's burning and the period of exile's duration this business is near to destroying me—the knife has reached the bone. My incapacity has arrived at its limit and weakness

46

has overcome me. And that secret (of my great love for you) has not remained behind the curtain as it was (since my suffering has become obvious to all). How could it remain so? How?

The door is locked, the veil thrown down; and the key, although hung upon the door, is behind the veil. There will be no rest until the curtains are lifted and the door of the house is opened. So is there any kind companion or sympathetic friend?

Separation—till when? Exile—how long?
Should I complain of my state to other than God?

O my master! Whoever leaves his people is an exile, and the exile's torment is severe. So, happy is he who has not been exiled from his Homeland and has not left the presence of Its inhabitants! Through gazing upon the lights of Its Essence, he is able to do without the lights of Its Attributes.[21] He travels, but he abides upon the carpet of contemplation. He traverses the way, moving [?] from place to place and light to light. He undergoes constant changes in the lights of the Names and Attributes. He goes beyond the stages of the spiritual climbing and ascent. But he is immobile, not moving, having no agitation. "Thou seest the mountains, that thou supposest fixed, passing by like clouds" (Koran XXVII:88).

So here we have a traveler with the Highest Friend within the paths of the eternities-without-beginning and the eternities-without-end. He undergoes constant changes with Him in the mornings and evenings, in keeping with His constant changes in States and circumstances.[22] The tongue of his spiritual state recites,

"I do not know what homelands we are passing by
    when He is with me.
How could the thought of any *place* be other than dis-
    tasteful to us?"

The possessor of this station—like you, my lord and master—needs no exile, nor does he content himself with any return. But as for him who has not reached this mighty station of contemplation—like this exile—he is always moving toward abandoning that within which he has appeared, and entering into that from which he has exited—"Surely unto God all things come home" (Koran XLII:53).

The tendencies of my temperament and the injunctions of the

INTRODUCTION

Shari'ah keep on inciting me to return to my original homeland and the mine of union, which is the radiant threshold and shining station of our lord. But whenever this uneasy one decides to return to that land and turn his face toward that sanctuary, some obstacle catches him by the skirt, and escape from it seems impossible.

> The waves of desire refuse all except nearness to you—
> But circumstances reject all except distance.

Each day my mind pulls me to one place, my heart draws me to another, the Shari'ah commands toward a perfection, and the Truth does what It will as It must. What can this poor soul do?

> He saw lightning in the east, so he yearned for the east.
> If it had sparked from the west, he would have yearned
> for the west.
> For my love is for the Friend and His people,
> My love is not for places and dirt. (Ibn al-'Arabi)

I hope that the magnetism of your all-vanquishing resolve will begin to attract and cause motion.

> The end of the tether is in your hand, and I am trained
> to the hand.
> When you pull me toward yourself, I will return to you.

> I have been so nearly destroyed by separation from you,
> That if you do not take my hand, I will never be able to
> stand up.

My resolve requests me to return, but my courtesy says, "Only if you are given permission." So the servant stands bewildered between the two. Look! What do you see? Is there then any way for union?

> Return! For I may have need of thee!

> Can it be you will say
>   "I shall see you in this world"
> and that again I may
>   sit with you a moment in joy?

48

that I shall hear with heart's ear
    your heart-expanding words?
that with spirit's eye I shall see
    your all-comforting face?
I am unworthy of you
    but—accept me,
take me for good or ill. What can I do?
    I am what I am.
Just once, pass this way—
    for I am pained with desire.
Spare one glance at my condition:
    wretched in the extreme.
Of my existence in this world
    not a trace would remain
if the hope of union with you
    did not sustain me with solace;
but now I am happy, with my last
    breath hovering at my lips,
yes, happy—because your lips
    are my own sweet soul.

The story is long, but life is short and I have not the strength to speak. Because of the indications of the Shaykh (Ibn al-'Arabi)—may God be well pleased with him[23]—I left Rum and came to the sanctuaries of Damascus and Jerusalem. From there I went on to the tomb of the Prophet in the Hijaz. Here I am awaiting further indications.

I gather that you are not coming to inquire after my state.

During sleep, then, at least send your image.

Since the compassion of your presence is general, I hope that for your servant it will be specific. May you continue to dwell in the station of perfecting the imperfect and elevating the words of the perfect. I ask for you the best, and that within you the Whole may become manifest—that Whole within which there is no whole and no part. Praise belongs to God.

*   *   *

INTRODUCTION

Although 'Iraqi sometimes traveled, as is shown by his letter to Qunawi, he spent most of his time in Turkey. He became quite well known, and attracted many disciples and devotees of his own. Among those who were drawn to him was Amir Mu'inuddin Parwanah, the administrator of Rum.[24] He had a great affection for the poet, and often urged him to choose some bit of land where a house might be built for him. 'Iraqi however resisted; carefree and detached as always, he busied himself with his own concerns. Finally Parwanah built him a hospice in Tokat. It is said that Parwanah would not count a day of his life as having really passed unless it included a visit to 'Iraqi.

One day, this same Amir Mu'inuddin came to visit 'Iraqi, bringing a few pieces of gold. The poet paid no attention to him, and the amir was somewhat put out. But 'Iraqi laughed and said, "You cannot deceive me with gold. Send for Hasan the Minstrel." Parwanah sent for him at once, but when the messenger tried to bring the singer away, a crowd of his admirers blocked their path. The messenger had to return without Hasan, and Parwanah ordered the governor of the province to punish the troublemakers. In the end, Hasan was sent to 'Iraqi, who came out to meet him in the presence of Parwanah and his entourage.

When Hasan and his friends saw how magnificently they were received, they were astonished, since they had expected punishment rather than honors. 'Iraqi embraced Hasan and served cool drinks with his own hands. Hasan kissed the dust before Parwanah, and was kindly treated. At last they reached the city, and alighted at 'Iraqi's hospice, where they began a ceremony of *sama'* (literally "audition": music and dance) that went on for three days. Many fine poems were recited, including this:

Love the phoenix cannot be trapped
nor in heaven or earth can it be named;

no one has yet discovered its address:
its desert holds not a single footprint.

The world drains the last drops from its cup
though itself it is not outside the glass;

dawn and dusk I caress its face, its tresses,
though where it is no day or night exists.

INTRODUCTION

Morning-breeze, if you pass its lane
I have no message for it but this:

My repose, who are my very life, without you
I can take no single breath at ease.

Everyone in this world wants something, but I
have no desire at all—except your lips;

from the moment my heart first fell into your locks
I've busied myself with nothing but lassos and snares.

How lucky to have a friend like you here below
(or Above) . . . The enemy hasn't a chance!

Inaugurate a romance then with 'Iraqi
even though he's unworthy of such a boon.

Eventually Hasan the Minstrel asked permission to depart, and, it is said, returned home laden with gifts.

Another day, when Parwanah called on 'Iraqi, he found that the Sufi had just gone out, and so he hurried after him. He found 'Iraqi in the street, where some children were leading him around by a string, which he held in his teeth, making him run hither and yon and otherwise gleefully tormenting him. When they saw Parwanah approach with his train, they fled. A few people who heard of this incident criticized 'Iraqi, but Parwanah defended him and silenced his detractors.

Once, as Parwanah was passing by a polo field, he found 'Iraqi, mallet in hand, playing with some youths. Parwanah offered to join the game, and asked, "What position shall I take?" Silently, 'Iraqi pointed to the road—and the amir went on.

One morning 'Iraqi left the hospice, and that night failed to return. Next day Parwanah and his companions searched everywhere for him, but found no trace. On the third day they heard that he had been seen, wandering in the hills outside the city. They set off to find him, and at last discovered him, strolling in circles in the snow, without turban or shoes. He was perspiring, despite the cold, and reciting this poem:

In the World-displaying Cup, at first
the image of all Creation was reflected.

INTRODUCTION

The Cup filled with Love's wine
    and the myriad imprints of all things took shape.
Each atom of these prints and images
showed forth a detail of the universe:
    one draught, and 100,000 cups,
    one drop, and 100,000 taverns.
Pass by these enslaving images
and all your troubles will vanish.
    Put aside these printed shapes
    and come to understand
that all this painted display is naught
but the false double seen by a cross-eyed fool.
    When in the midst of this astigmatic vision
    you see the face of the Painter Himself
you will understand that He alone exists
and all the others are but fancies and reflections.
    Do you desire that your heart and eyes
    be cooled with the light of this realization?
Then change your morals, transmute your qualities,
and when they have been transformed
    rush to the wineshop, for only there
    may your goal be reached at last.
Behold the half-drunk eyes of the saki
and then, as elegantly as you can
    drain a cup, lose your senses, forget
    all that can be unified or dispersed
and take a glance at the saki's eyes,
his drunken eyes: this, this is supreme:
    Look: the saki's face
    how it swells the soul,
    the saki's eternal face in the
    World-displaying Cup.
Love, Love is both wine and cup, Love
is a wine that puts all rivals under the table.
    That first World-displaying Cup is but
    a reflection of the purity of Love's glass
and the half-drunk glance of the saki also drinks
from this wine whose ultimate end is desire.
    This cup was drained, and from its outpouring
    the water of life drenched the world;

52

INTRODUCTION

from that water a bubble arose
and was called "The 18,000 Worlds."
    Look: what was the world's beginning?
    Watch: what will be its end:
that which derives from something else
may attain its desire and yet stay unsatisfied
    and any form that is blended with wine
    cannot remain still without wine for even a moment.
He who suffers a hangover still will finally
(but only after a time) fall drunk;
    joyous the heart of him who borrows
    pure wine from the Friend's lips even *now*.
You who have no news of this intoxicating vintage
(never for a second having stepped outside yourself)
    how long have you boiled the pot of love-madness
    there in your monastery—and still the stew is raw!
Now come to the tavern, for a few days
sit from morning to night;
    drink a toast to the desires of the friend of wine
    till you're drunk enough to see through *his* eyes:
        Look: the saki's face
        how it swells the soul,
        the saki's eternal face in the
        World-displaying Cup.
Before the being or nonbeing of the universe
before the "E" of God's decree—"Exist!"
    the Self-manifestation of Love asked from Love
    the manifestation of the letters of the Greatest Name.
Love lifted its finger instead of a pen,
licked it, then wrote without hesitation
    upon its palm a Name—such a Name!
    that Adam himself is its talisman-seal.
In the very shape of its letters, Being
and Temporality alike were contained.
    Love wrote, then read, then closed its hand
    and hid the word from the eyes of all strangers.
O seeker of this Greatest Name,
do you wish to know it now, for certain?
    Then find the key which unlocks the world
    which opens the seal of the talisman

and when at last you've unlocked the lid
you'll find that you yourself are that Name,
    that all is related to you
    both manifest meaning and secret Word—
the Name which is the essence of the Named.
If this is what you find, then carry on
    —if not, well, don't take yourself too seriously.
    Go, knock knock knock on the tavern door
and when at last they suddenly
swing wide the door, open your eyes, rejoice,
    Look: the saki's face
    how it swells the soul,
    the saki's eternal face in the
    World-displaying Cup . . .

After some time Parwanah and his men tried to persuade 'Iraqi to return to the city; but, as the account says, he kept on "bubbling and
boiling" (the poem goes on for five more stanzas). Despite their en-
treaties he refused to return on horseback, but when the Amir Mu'inuddin tried to dismount and walk with him (as a sign of respect) he
would not allow it. He sent the amir on ahead and eventually returned by himself. For three days afterwards he held *sama'* at the hospice.

One day 'Iraqi was overcome by ecstasy in the midst of the ritual
prayer. It is the usual practice (although not mandatory) to recite only
a short Arabic formula while making a prostration of a few seconds'
duration. But 'Iraqi remained bent over for a long period and while
doing so extemporized this Persian poem:

There came to Your street a gypsy beggar
    hoping for a welcome
and fell, poor soul, in the dust at Your door.
    But he went nowhere, nowhere at all;
whom should he visit? where should he flee?
    with his leg snapped by the hand of desire?
He came to Your door, for in earth and heaven
    he found no place but there—
and how shall a beggar leave the gate
    of a King empty-handed?

INTRODUCTION

Every second my eyes search Your face
    hungry for that blessed greeting
and from moment to moment my soul borrows
    subsistence from Your lips.
I searched here and there but found no corner
    to hide You but in my narrow heart.[25]
Every face I see without Your face
    seems to me nothing but a beginning;
Wherever I tangled my heart in someone's tresses
    I gave myself to a dragon;
I drowned in my separation but no one,
    no friend took my hand.
In the world's mirror I beheld nothing
    but the world-displaying picture of Your face
for indeed all things of the world but You
    seem mere echo or mirage.
My eyes saw nothing, no purity
    in the darkness of the world;
I returned again to Your door
    hoping, praying for some hand-out.
In the garden of Your love, 'Iraqi
    is but a songless bird.

Another day a dissolute and heedless drunkard, "headless and footless" as the expression has it, turned up at the door of 'Iraqi's private chambers. Unmannerly, he entered and plopped down at the head of the shaykh's prayer carpet, where he began making an awful ruckus. But the worse his language, the more kindly the poet spoke to him and tried to calm him. 'Iraqi's companions wanted to toss him out, but the shaykh forbade them. In order to show the necessity for humility before all of God's creatures, he rolled up his own robe as a pillow for the drunkard's head—and the rascal promptly vomited and spoiled the robe. When he finally awoke, 'Iraqi himself washed his face and hands, and then ordered the servant to give him a hundred gold dirhams. To carry home the symbolical nature of physical drunkenness, which in certain ways illustrates the characteristics of spiritual intoxication,[26] he recited this poem:

Those who are drunk and ruined will find at this tavern
a treasure unearned in the prayers of a hundred elders.

INTRODUCTION

Do you wish to discover this treasure without pain?
Then sift each morning the dust at the tavern door.

If an atom of that dust should fall in your eye
you will encounter a hundred thousand suns

and if you suddenly catch the beam of light from a glass
at once you will find a goblet-full of illumination.

In selfless drunkenness you will find a place
where words are erased, all trace of allusion lost;

if you cannot lose yourself you'll never find this place.
Who finds such a state? Who finds such exalted station?

How long will you stick with the monastery's worshipful
habits?
For the prisoner of habit, obedience and self-denial are but
disbelief.

As long as you cannot jump free of your own embrace
your worship is bound to a temple of devilish idols.

Pawn your soul at the tavern to buy one sip
but do not try to trade on piety—the coin is debased.

How long will you stand dry-lipped on the shore of desire?
Hurl yourself—now!—into the infinite sea

that the traceless ocean may wash away all trace
and the shark of ecstasy swallow you in one bite.

When 'Iraqi is drowned, he'll find eternal life
and behold the secret of the Unseen in the world of the
Witness.

It would be gratifying to be able to record that, after this treatment,
the drunkard repented and became 'Iraqi's disciple, but the account
says no more.

One of 'Iraqi's followers was a wealthy Persian merchant named
Khwajah Zaynuddin Kashani. It happened once that he placed before
the shaykh a sack containing a thousand dinars; but 'Iraqi went on
chatting as if he had not noticed it. Now among 'Iraqi's friends was a
Christian priest, who used to visit the shaykh every fortnight or so,

when they would spend an evening alone together. Just at this moment, the priest walked in and placed *two* sacks of gold before the shaykh. Laughing, 'Iraqi at once picked up one of these sacks and set it beside the merchant's sack, saying, "Take these, and imagine you bought the leather and sent it to Tabriz."

The merchant blushed furiously, and with a thousand stammered apologies prostrated at 'Iraqi's feet. "O Shaykh!" he wept, "do not reject this base soul!" 'Iraqi replied, "Not at all. The best thing in the present situation is for you to take the gold"; and so saying, he pressed the two sacks on the merchant and sent him away.

When the merchant had gone, the disciples asked 'Iraqi, "How is it that you refused the money of the merchant, who after all is a Moslem, but accepted the gift of the Christian priest?" 'Iraqi answered, "Gold is the beloved of our merchant, and for its sake he travels from city to city and suffers much pain. He brought his beloved before me, but I did not think it right to separate him from it; nor would it have been kind to send him away without a profit."

The next day, one of the disciples met the merchant in the bazaar and asked him, "What was the real reason for the shaykh's refusing your money?" He explained, "Yesterday when I set out to see our master, I was carrying the gold, and happened to pass by the market. I noticed someone offering an excellent bargain in leather; at once I realized that it would be extremely profitable to use the thousand dinars to buy leather and send it to Tabriz where I know it could be sold for two thousand. I agonized over whether to do it or not, and finally overcame the temptation. But naturally the shaykh realized everything!"

At this time, Rum was ruled by the Mongol emperor Abaka. All manner of struggle and intrigue was going on between Abaka and the Mameluke emperor in Cairo, Baybars. Amir Mu'inuddin Parwanah, who owed allegiance to the Mongol Abaka, was caught between these two contending giants.

At the battle of Albistan in 675/1277, the Mongol forces—including Parwanah's contingent—were routed by the Mamelukes, and Parwanah's son was taken prisoner and sent to Cairo. Five days later Baybars entered Kaiseri and had himself crowned emperor of Rum according to the old Seljuk rituals. Parwanah fled to the family fief in Tokat. Baybars, however, feared a Mongol counterattack and withdrew to Egypt. The Mongol emperor Abaka suspected Parwanah of collaboration with Baybars, and ordered him to appear at court.[27]

INTRODUCTION

Parwanah knew he had fallen from favor. That night, he came to 'Iraqi and brought with him a purse full of precious jewels. He laid it before the poet, saying, "This is all the wealth I have saved during my term of office. Now they are seeking my life; fortune has turned against me." 'Iraqi wept, and Parwanah also lamented. After a while the nobleman recovered and said, "You know that my beloved son is in prison in Cairo. If you pass that way after my death, use these jewels to try to secure his release. If you succeed, do not let him out of your sight for a moment, but make him your dervish and kill in him all ambition for secular power. If however they will not release him, spend the money in any way you see fit."

'Iraqi threw the purse in a corner. Parwanah bade him farewell and left to meet his fate. The Mongol emperor ordered him executed, and he was killed in Rabi' I 676/August 1277. The whole of Anatolia was now thrown into disorder, and much of the area fell under the control of wild Turkoman tribes. Abaka therefore sent his brother Kangirtay, along with the vizier Shamsuddin Juwayni (brother of the famous historian), to consolidate Mongol rule in the province. They quickly regained Tokat, Konya, and other cities.[28]

With Juwayni traveled a group of outstanding religious scholars. When they arrived at Tokat, one of these scholars—Mawlana Aminuddin Hajji Bulah—entered the city and at sundown reached the hospice of 'Iraqi. Turning his horse over to a servant he entered the house, where he found the poet saying the evening prayer. Mawlana joined him at his devotions, and afterwards introduced himself. They sat down together and began to discuss matters concerning the spiritual Path; and before they knew it, half the night had passed.

"I was so fascinated by meeting you", said 'Iraqi, "and so enchanted by your conversation, that I have quite forgotten to prepare supper for you!" "Never mind," Mawlana answered; "I have a saddle-bag of food with me." And he asked the servant to bring it in. They ate some halwah and cakes with great relish, then prayed the midnight prayer and retired to sleep.

Mawlana remained with 'Iraqi for three days, and they greatly enjoyed each other's company and talk. As it happens, one of the reasons for Mawlana's visit to the city was to try to discover where the late Parwanah had hidden his wealth. All the time they talked, the purse of jewels lay in the corner; but both of them were emptied of this world and all it contains.

At last Mawlana returned to the Mongol camp. Juwayni demanded of him, "Have you grown tired of us? It is three days since you disappeared!" "God forbid!" Mawlana replied; "but I was visiting Shaykh Fakhruddin 'Iraqi. What sweet sherbets I tasted at his tavern! and what words I heard there, such as I have never heard before! If the desire to return to you and the other friends had not overcome me, I would happily have spent the rest of my life with that wonderful man." Juwayni declared, "I must meet this person. Do you think it would be proper for me to come to him, or more appropriate for him to come to us?" Mawlana replied that 'Iraqi should be invited to the camp; an invitation was sent along with a mule for the poet to ride, and the vizier and his friends showered the poet with honors. He in turn regaled the company with talk of the mystic Way. His words grew warm, and his eloquence brought tears to Juwayni's eyes.

Meanwhile however, spies and informers had been at work. A group of the envious had gone to Prince Kangirtay and poisoned his ears against 'Iraqi. They reported that Parwanah had turned over the entire treasury of Rum to the Sufi poet, rather than merely his own personal fortune. As soon as Juwayni returned to the prince's presence, Kangirtay told him that a group of soldiers had been sent to arrest 'Iraqi.

Juwayni, however, had no intention of allowing 'Iraqi to be killed, and he acted much more quickly than the arresting party. He sent word to 'Iraqi that his life was in danger, and advised him to flee. He included with the message a sack of a thousand dinars, adding that he hoped it would help defray the expenses of the journey. "In any case," he ended, "depart now, in any safe direction."

Tired as he was of Tokat, which had become the scene of such upheaval, 'Iraqi did not care to end his life there; and as soon as he heard this message he at once arose, picked up the purse of jewels and the sack of dinars, selected two of his companions, mounted the mule Juwayni had sent him, and set out for Sinope.[29] From there he went on to Egypt.

On his arrival in Cairo, 'Iraqi took lodgings at the Salihiyyah hospice, where he rested for three days. He then began his search for Parwanah's son, intending to plan his release, but found no way of doing so. At last, he took the purse of jewels and presented himself at the gate of the sultan's palace, where he begged for an audience.[30]

The sultan heard of this. He ordered the guards to search the dervish for weapons and then admit him. Finding him unarmed, they brought him to the throne room, where he bowed to the sultan, laid the purse at the foot of the throne, and stood up again. The sultan gazed upon him and realized at once that he was dealing with an exceptional man. He asked 'Iraqi to be seated, and then inquired as to the significance of the purse. "It is a trust," 'Iraqi replied. "I do not know what is in it." The sultan signed for the purse to be examined; it was, of course, found to be full of jewels of incredible value. 'Iraqi explained how he had been given the purse by Parwanah, and told the whole story from beginning to end. The sultan was astounded that any man, with such wealth in his hands, should have delivered it all without taking anything for himself. The shaykh, realizing what the sultan was thinking, recited the Koranic Verse, "Say, the goods of this world are of little worth: the world to come is better for him who fears God, and ye shall not be wronged an iota" (IV:77).

Now the sultan was even more amazed, and leaving his throne he came and sat down before 'Iraqi and listened to his discourse. That day, it is said, he wept more than in all his life before. He commanded Parwanah's son to be released; he treated the youth with affection, and gave him the rank of prince, a personal bodyguard of two men, and a daily stipend of a hundred dirhams. As for 'Iraqi, he appointed him chief shaykh of Cairo, and commanded that on the next day all the Sufis and divines should attend the court in honor of the occasion.

So next morning a thousand dervishes, as well as all the religious scholars and notables of Cairo, watched as the sultan mounted 'Iraqi on his own horse, and clothed him in a robe and hood of honor. He arranged that 'Iraqi alone be mounted, and that all the others, nobles, scholars, and generals alike, should walk at his stirrup.

When 'Iraqi saw all this, the thought suddenly entered his head that no other man of the age had ever been treated with such respect. At once he realized that he was in danger of being overcome by his ego. Immediately he ripped off his hood and turban and placed them on the saddle before him. The crowd watched in stunned silence as he sat there, till, after a few minutes, he picked up the turban and hood and put them back on his head.

The crowd began to titter. "How could such a man deserve such rank?" whispered someone. "He is a madman!" "A buffoon!"; and all of them began to ridicule him. "Why did you do such a thing?" demanded the vizier; but 'Iraqi answered, "Hold your tongue! What do you know?"

News of this scandal was at once carried to the sultan. Next day he sent for 'Iraqi and asked for an explanation. "My carnal soul overcame me," the poet replied. "If I had not acted in that way, I should never have escaped from the consequences of my sin." This incident only increased the sultan's faith in him, and he doubled 'Iraqi's pension.

After some time in Cairo, 'Iraqi decided to leave for Damascus. Perhaps Ibn al-'Arabi had once again come to him in a dream, calling him to himself, but this time for a far longer stay. When the sultan heard of this, he summoned him and tried to persuade him not to go. 'Iraqi won him over, however; and the sultan asked only that he remain till arrangements for the journey be made. But since 'Iraqi would not delay, the sultan ordered messenger pigeons to be sent, so that at each station along the route the poet might be received with honor. He also wrote to the Malik al-umara' ("king of amirs") of Damascus, advising him of the shaykh's visit, and saying that all the scholars, Sufis, and notables of Damascus should be sent out to meet him; that he should be appointed chief shaykh of the district; and that a regular allowance should be paid to his servants. All happened as the Sultan commanded, and the populace of Damascus greeted 'Iraqi with warmth.

Six months later 'Iraqi's son Kabiruddin arrived from Multan. Although he had been sitting in the seat of Baha'uddin Zakariyya',[31] he felt drawn by filial love, and left India to the great regret of the brethren there, who would have prevented his departure, but for a dream in which it was revealed to them that they must allow him to go.

So Kabiruddin enjoyed for a time his father's company. But then 'Iraqi was stricken with a fatal illness: a bloody swelling of the face. He slept for five days, and on the sixth called for his son and companions. He bade them farewell with tears in his eyes, and recited the verse, "The day on which a man shall flee from his brother, and his mother, and his father" (LXXX:34–35). Then he spoke this quatrain:

When by Decree this world was first begun
not after Adam's want the deed was done;
    but of the portion on that Day assigned
none shall win more, nor any less hath won.[32]

So he conversed with them awhile, till at last he drank the cup of fate and passed from this transitory realm to the eternal shore. The Malik al-umara' and the people of Damascus all gathered to pay their last

INTRODUCTION

respects to the dead, and with much lamentation buried him in the Salihiyyah cemetery, beside the tomb of Ibn al-'Arabi. For three days they mourned, and on the fourth appointed his son Kabiruddin his successor. When he in turn passed over to the divine mercy, they buried him at his father's side.

It is said that 'Iraqi died at the age of seventy-eight, on the eighth of Dhu-l-Qa'dah, 688 (November 23, 1289). Travelers have reported that when the Damascenes visit the tomb they say of Ibn al-'Arabi, "This is the ocean of the Arabs"; and of 'Iraqi, "This is the ocean of the Persians".[33]

NOTES

1. Except where otherwise noted, this version of 'Iraqi's "Life" is based on that given in the introduction to many manuscripts of 'Iraqi's *Diwan* and printed in the *Kulliyyat-i 'Iraqi*, ed. S. Nafisi, 3d ed. (Tehran, 1338/1959), pp. 46–65. So far as is known, this is the oldest and most complete account of his life, probably written shortly after his death in 688/1289, and certainly composed before 857/1453, the date of Ms. Fatih 3844. All significant accounts of his life that have come down to us are based on this source. A. J. Arberry made use of parts of it in his "Biography," in his translation of 'Iraqi's *'Ush-shaq-namah* or *Dah-namah* [The song of lovers] (Oxford, 1939).

2. After the region of Persia called 'Iraq-i 'ajam, not after the country of Iraq. Certain authorities say the name of the Persian region should be transliterated as 'Araq, and thus the name of the poet as 'Araqi.

3. The Islamic sciences are divided into those that one can learn only by transmission from others (*al-'ulum an-naqliyyah*), such as the Koran, the *hadith* or sayings of the Prophet, jurisprudence, and Arabic grammar; and those that can be discovered independently by man's intellect (*al-'ulum al-'aqliyyah*), such as mathematics, the natural sciences, and philosophy.

4. Throughout Islamic history many Sufis have taken to heart the Koranic command, "Journey in the land!" (III:137, etc.). They took this outward journeying as complementary to the inward, spiritual journeying on the Sufi path. For "in the land are signs for those having sure faith; and in yourselves; what, do you not see?" (Koran, LI:21); and "We shall show them Our signs in the horizons and in themselves" (XLI:53). Since such Sufis had dedicated themselves to God and trusted only in Him, they tended to ignore all outward, socially accepted norms, so long as ignoring them did not involve breaking the Shari'ah, or Divine law. If long beards were signs of honorable social standing, they would shave theirs off. They dressed colorfully and carried various implements, such as begging bowls and axes, to set themselves apart from ordinary people. These Sufis came to be known as *"qalandars"* or Kalandars.

INTRODUCTION

But the situation of the Kalandars is complicated by the fact that social outcasts, attracted by this outwardly "irresponsible" mode of life, often dressed like the Kalandars and traveled from city to city. However, they would take every opportunity to break the Shari'ite statutes on such matters as wine-drinking and fornication. Because people unconnected with Sufism could see little apparent difference between the two groups, they called them all "Kalandars" indiscriminately. Since one of the spiritual attitudes cultivated by the Kalandars is that summarized by Christ's words, "Beware of practicing your piety before men in order to be seen by them" (Mt. 6:1), many Kalandars did not mind the notoriety they gained by the activities of this second group. Some of them (in particular the Sufis known as *malamatiyyah*) actually did what they could to help foster their irreligious image, again, as long as this did not necessitate transgressing the statutes of the Divine law.

5. The titles represent some of the standard textbooks in the Islamic sciences: *at-Tafsir al-kabir*, an authoritative commentary on the Koran by the celebrated theologian Fakhruddin ar-Razi (d. 606/1209); *al-Isharat wa-t-tanbihat* by the most famous of the Moslem philosophers, Abu 'Ali ibn Sina (d. 428/1037); *Ma'alim at-tanzil*, a Koranic commentary by Hasan ibn Mas'ud al-Farra' al-Baghawi (d. 510/1117); *al-Hawi* on medicine by Muhammad ibn Zakariyya' ar-Razi (d. 313/925 or 323/935); *Jami' ad-daqa'iq fi kashf al-haqa'iq* on logic by Najmuddin 'Ali ibn 'Umar, known as Dabiran al-Katibi al-Qazwini (d. 650/1252–1253); and *Rawdat al-munajjimin* on astronomy by Shahmardan ibn Abi-l-Khayr ar-Razi (fl. fifth/eleventh c.).

6. J. A. Subhan, *Sufism: Its Saints and Shrines*, rev. ed. (Lucknow, 1960), pp. 239–242.

7. Islam's view of music has always been slightly ambiguous. To summarize a long and involved discussion, one can say that since music stimulates a person's natural disposition, and since the majority are disposed toward the desires of the individual, passionate soul (*nafs*), it is in the best interest of the community for music to be forbidden to the majority. To express such a conditional prohibition in legalistic terms, the Shari'ah is forced to forbid music to society as such, all the while leaving enough question and doubt about this prohibition so that those with a spiritual disposition can avail themselves of the support music provides without committing a transgression. Hence the Sufis have often made use of music in their gatherings. Thus we can say that the music referred to here in 'Iraqi's biography is, on the surface, forbidden by the letter of the Shari'ah, but it is tolerated by many of the *'ulama'* because of its ambiguous nature and the impossibility in practice of discerning between those who should be allowed to listen to it and those who should not. See S. H. Nasr, "The Influence of Sufism on Traditional Persian Music," in *The Sword of Gnosis*, ed. J. Needleman (Baltimore: Penguin Books, 1974), pp. 330–342; also idem, "Islam and Music," *Studies in Comparative Religion*, Winter 1976, pp. 37–45.

8. 'Iraqi's *Kulliyyat* is about 400 pages in its modern edition.

INTRODUCTION

9. Translated, not very elegantly, by Arberry; see note 1.

10. This would probably have been either Balban or his son Muhammad Shah, who was governor of Multan and reputed to have been a drunkard (*Sufism: Its Saints and Shrines,* pp. 242–243).

11. The leadership of the Order in Multan passed to Baha'uddin Zakariyya's eldest son, Sadruddin (d. 684/1285). On receiving his inheritance, which consisted of land and "seven lakhs of gold mohars," Sadruddin at once gave it all away to the poor. When a friend criticized him for throwing away what his father had so carefully amassed, Sadruddin retorted, "But my father had complete control over all worldly desires, and so could afford to keep such wealth, whereas I am weak, and therefore fear lest worldly possessions should make me forget God" (ibid., p. 242).

12. B. Furuzanfar, *Risalah dar tahqiq-i ahwal wa zindigani-yi Mawlana Jalaluddin Mahmud,* second printing (Tehran 1333/1954), pp. 124–125.

13. On Qunawi see W. Chittick, "The Last Will and Testament," pp. 43–58; also *Ascendant Stars.*

14. See B. M. Weischer and P. L. Wilson, *Heart's Witness: The Sufi Quatrains of Awhaduddin Kermani* (Tehran, 1978).

15. See A. J. Arberry's translation: *The Poem of the Way* (London, 1952).

16. See R. J. W. Austin's translation in the present series; also, the English translation of T. Burckhardt's partial French translation: *The Wisdom of the Prophets* (Gloucestershire, 1975).

17. See A. J. Arberry's translation of an-Niffari's work, *The Mawaqif and Mukhatabat* (London, 1935).

18. See W. Chittick, "The Last Will and Testament"; for more details on these figures see Chittick, *Ascendant Stars.*

19. Shamsuddin Maghribi (d. 809/1406–1407) and Mahmud Shabistari (d. 720/1320), among many others, were directly indebted to 'Iraqi. Jami wrote a commentary on the *Lama'at* and is directly influenced by both its style and content in such works as the *Lawami'* and the *Lawa'ih* (the latter was translated by E. H. Whinfield and M. M. Kazvini [London, 1914]).

20. Our translation is based on a collation of two early manuscripts, each of which is so illegible as to be practically useless without the other: Esad Ef. 1783/f. 86 (Suleymaniye Library) and Mevlana Muzesi 1633/ff. 112–3 (Konya). The authenticity of the letter cannot be doubted. Both manuscripts are contained in collections of letters to and from Qunawi. The Esad Ef. collection accompanies Qunawi's long philosophical correspondence with Nasir al-Din Tusi, while the Mevlana Muzesi collection is appended to a copy of Qunawi's *an-Nafahat.* The fact that the order of the letters is different in each collection, that the Mevlana Muzesi collection is much longer, and that each manuscript accompanies different works all serve to show that the two collections of letters represent separate and ancient lines of transmission. Finally, the style of 'Iraqi's letter is practically identical with that of the *Lama'at,* the

long poem is also found in his *Diwan* (p. 241), and there is no reason anyone would want to fabricate such a document.

21. The manner in which 'Iraqi speaks about his own exile from Qunawi and then without warning refers to the symbolism of the situation by discussing the prototype of all of man's exiles, i.e., his distance from God, is typical of his writings, both his poetry and prose. For him each phenomenon in the world is an immediate and tangible "sign" (*ayah*) of God, an instance that recalls the phenomenon's ontological prototype.

22. 'Iraqi is referring to one of Ibn al-'Arabi's famous teachings: that the Sufi's heart (*qalb*) is constantly transformed (*taqallub*) by spiritual states, since it is the locus of God's never-repeating theophanies. Just as "Every day"— and, says Jandi, with God a "day" is an "instant"—"God is in a State" (Koran LV:29), so every instant the Sufi undergoes a new transformation, "therein glorifying Him, in the mornings and the evenings" (XXIV:36). See T. Izutsu, "The Concept of Perpetual Creation in Islamic Mysticism and Zen Buddhism," in *Melanges offerts à Henry Corbin*, ed. S. H. Nasr (Tehran, 1977), especially pp. 136–141.

23. At this time Ibn al-'Arabi had been dead for many years. But the fact that after mentioning the "shaykh," 'Iraqi adds a prayer reserved only for the dead, and that in referring to him as "*the* shaykh" to Qunawi he must mean someone whom Qunawi would refer to by the same title, shows that 'Iraqi in fact can only mean Ibn al-'Arabi himself. It was common for Sufis to see living or deceased masters in dreams or visions and to act according to their instructions. So from the context we understand that Ibn al-'Arabi had asked 'Iraqi to come visit him at his tomb in Damascus. This incident is particularly significant in light of the fact that 'Iraqi is buried in Damascus next to Ibn al-'Arabi.

24. For some notes on him, see E. G. Browne's *Literary History of Persia* (London, 1902–1924), vol. 3, p. 106.

25. An allusion to the *hadith* in which God says, "My heaven and earth embrace Me not, but the heart of My gentle, meek, believing servant does embrace Me."

26. In his *Lawami'* Jami summarizes the teachings of Ibn al-'Arabi's school concerning the reason wine is taken as a symbol for spiritual intoxication under ten headings. See W. C. Chittick, "Jami on Divine Love and the Image of Wine," *Studies in Mystical Literature 1* (1981): pp. 193–209.

27. C. Cahen, *Pre-Ottoman Turkey* (London, 1968), pp. 288–291.

28. Ibid., p. 291.

29. Sinope at this time was ruled by Mu'inuddin Muhammad, one of Parwanah's sons. Qunawi's disciple Jandi dedicated his commentary on the *Fusus* to this ruler, who must have shared his father's interest in Sufism (see, for example, Mss. Kiliç, Ali Paşa 606 and Şehid Ali Paşa 1241). He also dedicated his *Nafhat ar-ruh wa tuhfat al-futuh* to a "pious princess" from Sinope

INTRODUCTION

(Tehran Univ. Central Library 2393), who was probably Parwanah's daughter or granddaughter.

30. Although Nafisi, the editor of 'Iraqi's *Kulliyyat*, suggests that this was Baybars, in fact it must have been al-Mansur Sayf al-Din Kalaun, who ruled from 678/1279 to 689/1289. As Nafisi himself points out, Kangirtay's campaign to Rum took place in 680/1281–1282 and he died in 681/1282–1283. Even if the campaign took place before this date, 'Iraqi could not have reached Egypt by 676/1277, the year Baybars died. Since his stay there was an extended one and the "sultan" seems to remain the same person, he could not be one of the two other sultans who ruled in the two years separating Baybars from Kalaun.

31. So says the account; see however note 11.

32. Arberry's translation, with a few changes.

33. Any trace of 'Iraqi's grave seems to have been erased in the middle of the tenth/sixteenth century, perhaps when Sultan Selim restored Ibn al-'Arabi's tomb. Reports from the beginning of that century refer to 'Iraqi's grave, but by the end of the century, people no longer write about having visited it (Nafisi, *Kulliyyat-i 'Iraqi*, p. 43).

Divine Flashes

In the name of God,
Merciful and Compassionate
Refuge we Seek in Him

PROLOGUE

Praise belongs to God Who made effulgent the face of
His Friend Muhammad with Beauty's theophanies, that
it sparkled with light:

beholding therein the far reach of Perfection, filling
Him with Joy at the sight.

God began with him, loved him with untainted love,
even then,

when Adam was not yet remembered nor the Tablet
yet traced by the Pen.

So in the warehouse of Existence he is the treasure,
the key to unlock Generosity's sealed chest;

he is both the niche and goal of the ecstatic wanderer,
and the very ecstasy in his breast.

He owns the Banner of Praise, he owns the Laudable
Station

and from the tongue of that spiritual rank there
flows forth in recitation:

> Truly in form
> I am Adam's son—
> and yet

DIVINE FLASHES

within Adam himself
    lies a secret—
my secret—
    that testifies:
I am his father! (Ibn al-Farid)

"Outwardly" he says "I am of Adam's children
yet in every way far above him in station.
I gaze at the glass which reveals my beauty
and see the universe but an image of that image.
In the paradise of theophany I am the Sun: marvel not
that every atom becomes a vehicle of my manifestation.
What are the Holy Spirits? the delegates of my secret;
and the shapes of men? the vessels of my bodily form.
World-encircling Ocean? a drop of my overflowing effusion;
purest Light? but a spark of my illumination.
No, *I am Light:* All things are seen in my unveiling
and from moment to moment my radiance is more manifest.
The Divine Names bear their fruit in me. Look:
I am the mirror of the shining Essence.
These lights which arise from the East of Nothingness
are myself, every one—yet I am more.
From the Throne to the outstretched carpet of the world
all things are motes in the sun-ray of my illumined mind.
The world would shed its darkness in my bright being
if I tore the curtain from my attributes.
What is the water which gave life to undying Khezr?
a drop from my Spring of Abundance.[1]
And that breath of Christ which brought the dead to life?
One breath of my breath, the nurture of Spirits.
My essence? the locus of theophany of all the Names . . .
No. When I look in truth, I am the Greatest Name."

Then God benedict him and his Household,
the prophets and righteous, martyrs and virtuous!

But now to our intent: a few words explaining the way-stations
of Love in the tradition of *The Sparks;* in tune with the voice of each
spiritual state as it passes, I shall dictate them as a mirror to reflect
every lover's Beloved. But how high is Love, too high for us to circle

DIVINE FLASHES

the Kaaba of its Majesty on the strength of mere understanding, mere words; too exalted for us to gaze upon its real beauty with eye unveiled and vision direct:

> Removed is Love above man's aspiration,
> above the tales of union and separation;
>
> for that which transcends the imagination
> escapes all metaphor and explication.

Love lies hid in Power's pavilion, unique in the perfection of unneedfulness. The very veils of its Essence are its Attributes—but these Attributes are enfolded in its Essence. Its Majesty yearns for its own Beauty—yet its Beauty is embodied in its Majesty. Without cease Love loves itself, pays no heed to other than itself. Each moment it raises the veil from some darling's face, each breath it begins a lover's melody:

> Love plays its lute behind the screen—
> where is a lover to listen to its tune?
>
> With every breath a new song,
> each split second a new string plucked.
>
> The world has spilled Love's secret—
> when could music ever hold its tongue?
>
> Every atom babbles the mystery—
> Listen yourself, for I'm no tattletale!

Now and now with every tongue Love whispers its secrets to its own ears; now and now with every ear it hears the murmuring of its own tongue. In every blink of every eye it shows forth its loveliness to its own sight; at every wink, here and there it reveals its existence to its own contemplation. Listen to me and I shall describe it:

> It speaks to me in the silence of this one
> then through the words of that one speaking;
>
> it whispers to me through an eyebrow raised
> and the message of an eye winking.

71

DIVINE FLASHES

And do you know what words it breathes into my ear? It says,

"I am Love: in heaven and earth I have no place;
I am the Wondrous Phoenix whose spoor cannot be traced.

With eyebrow-bow and arrow-winks I hunt
both worlds—and yet my weapons cannot be found.

Like the sun I brighten each atom's cheek;
I cannot be pinpointed: I am too manifest.

I speak with every tongue, listen with all ears,
but marvel at this: My ears and tongue are erased.

Since in all the world only I exist
above and below, no likeness of me can be found."

INTRODUCTION

Know that in each of these *Flashes* we make allusion to a reality purified of all entification. Call it Amourousness or Love, let us not quarrel over words. We here recount the nature of its degrees and phases, its journey through stages of repose and lodging, its appearance in meanings and realities, its manifestation in the vestments of Beloved and lover, the passing away of the lover's entity in that of the Beloved, the seclusion of the Beloved's properties in those of the lover, and the enwrapment of both in Love's overpowering Oneness. Here, in this last, all separation is at-oned, all rips sewn up, light hidden in Light: manifestation nonmanifest in Manifestation. From within the tents of Power comes this call:

"All other than God, is it not *vanitas?*
All joys fleeting, vanishing?

They go forth unto God, the One, All-subjugating (XIV:48).[2]
All creatures disappear, no description, no trace remains."

DIVINE FLASHES

FLASH I

*On the fact that Love is the origin of
the lover and the Beloved, how these two grow out of
Love in the First Entification, and how each of them
is in need of the other[3]*

"Lover" and "Beloved" are derived from "Love," but Love upon Its mighty Throne is purified of all entification, in the sanctuary of Its Reality too holy to be touched by inwardness or outwardness. Thus, that It might manifest Its perfection (a perfection identical both with Its own Essence and Its own Attributes), It showed Itself to Itself in the looking-glass of "lover" and "Beloved." It displayed Its own loveliness to Its own eyes, and became viewer and viewed; the names "lover" and "Beloved," the attributes of seeker and Sought, then appeared. When Love revealed the Outward to the Inward, It made the lover's fame; when It embellished the Inward with the Outward, It made known the Beloved's name.

> Other than that Essence
>   not one atom existed;
> when It manifested Itself
>   these "others" came to life.
> O Thou Whose Outward is "lover,"
>   Whose Inward is "Beloved"!
> Who has ever seen
>   Sought become seeker? ('Attar)

By means of "Beloved," Love became the mirror of "lover" that It might study Itself in that glass; by means of "lover" It became the mirror of "Beloved" that It might behold therein Its Names and Attributes. To the eye of true Witness, no more than One is to be seen— but since this One Face shows Itself in two mirrors, each mirror will display a different face.

> But one face:
>   multiply the mirrors,
>   make It many.

73

DIVINE FLASHES

No other shows its face
    for each thing that exists
is the same as the One
    come into manifestation. ('Attar)

FLASH II

On the Perfection of Distinct-Manifestation,
which is the Self-Revelation of God in the loci of theophany
and manifestation and which arises from
the Second Entification

    King Love desired to pitch His tent in the desert, open the door
of His warehouse, and scatter treasures to the world;

        then raised His parasol,
            hoisted His banners
      to mingle Being
          and nothingness.
      Ah, the restlessness
          of enrapturing Love
      has thrown the world
          in tumult!

But if He had not done so, the world would have slumbered on, at
rest with existence and nonexistence, at ease in the Retreat of Vision
where "God was, and nothing was with Him" (H).[4]

      In those days
          before a trace
      of the two worlds,
          no "other" yet imprinted
      on the Tablet of Existence,
          I, the Beloved, and Love
      lived together
          in the corner
      of an uninhabited
          cell.

DIVINE FLASHES

But suddenly Love the Unsettled flung back the curtain from the whole show, to display Its perfection as the "Beloved" before the entity of the world;

and when Its ray of loveliness appeared
at once the world came into being
at once the world borrowed sight
from Love's Beauty, saw the loveliness of Its Face
and at once went raving mad;
borrowed sugar from Love's lips
and tasting it at once began to speak.

One needs Thy Light
To see Thee.

The splendor of Beauty bestowed upon the lover's entity a light with which that very Beauty might be seen; for only through It can It be perceived. Or, as the Arabs say, "No one carries their gifts but their horses."

When the lover grasped the joy of this Witnessing he caught the taste of existence. He heard the whispered command—"BE!"[5]—and dancing to Love's tavern door he exclaimed,

"O saki, fill a cup
with that wine:
my heart, my religion
my sweet life.
Can drinking be my liturgy?
Then my Faith
will be to sip the Beloved
from this chalice.

Then in an instant the saki poured so much Existence-wine into that Nothingness-cup

that because of the wine's pureness
and the crystal clarity of the glass
the color of glass and wine were confused.
All is glass—or, no, all is wine.

DIVINE FLASHES

All is wine—or, no, all is glass!
When the sky is tainted
with the colors of the sun
heaven kicks away the blankets and sheets,
the shadows of nothingness. Day and Night
make peace with each other:
thus have the world's affairs been ordered.

The Morning of Manifestation sighed, the breeze of Grace breathed gently, ripples stirred upon the sea of Generosity. The clouds of Effusion poured down the rain of "He sprinkled creation with His Light" (H) upon the soil of preparedness; so much rain that *the earth shone with the Light of its Lord* (XXXIX:69). The lover, then, satiated with the water of life, awoke from the slumber of nonexistence, put on the cloak of being and tied round his brow the turban of contemplation; he cinched the belt of desire about his waist and set forth with the foot of sincerity upon the path of the Search.

He came from theory to actuality,
from hearsay to the Embrace! (Sana'i)

As soon as he opened his eyes his gaze fell upon the Beloved, and he said, "I have never beheld anything without seeing God before it" ('Ali); he looked at himself, found that all of him was HE, and exclaimed,

"So only Reality peers out of my eyes!

A peculiar business, indeed!

If I have become the Beloved,
who is the lover?"

Here indeed the lover is the very Beloved, for he has no existence of his own to call "the lover." He still sleeps in his original nonexistence, just as the Beloved remains forever in His Eternity: "He is now as He was."[6]

Beloved, Love and lover—three-in-one.
There is no place for Union here
so what's this talk of "separation"?

DIVINE FLASHES

FLASH III

On the Perfection of Distinct-Vision,
which is His Direct-Vision of Himself in the loci of theophany
and manifestation, and the states which are
subordinate to this Direct-Vision

Now though Love was forever admiring Itself through Itself, It also wished to study the perfect beauty of Its Belovedness in some mirror. Peering into the glass of the lover's reality, It saw Its own face, and wondered,

> Is it you or I,
> this reality in the eye?
> Beware, beware
> of the word "two"! (al-Hallaj)

It fell in love with Its own reflection, and bruited about the world the clatter of *He loves them and they love Him* (V:54). Look closely and you will see that

> the painter's fascination
> is with his own canvas.
> There's no one else about
> so ... rejoice!

The sun shines in the moon's mirror, but the moon contains naught of the sun's essence. Just so, in Love's Essence there is naught but HE, nor is there aught of His Essence in anything other-than-He. As sunlight is attributed to the moon, so is the Beloved's form ascribed to the lover; but in truth

> each image painted
> on the canvas of existence
> is the form
> of the artist himself.
> Eternal Ocean
> spews forth new waves.
> "Waves" we call them;
> but there is only the Sea.

DIVINE FLASHES

Many and disparate waves do not make the sea a multiplicity; no more do the Names make the Named more than One. When the sea breathes they call it mist; when mist piles up they call it clouds. It falls again, they name it rain; it gathers itself and rejoins the sea. And it is now the same sea it ever was.

> So Ocean is Ocean
> as it was in Eternity,
> contingent beings
> but its waves and currents.
> Do not let the ripples
> and mists of the world
> veil you from Him
> who takes form within these veils. (Jandi)

Beginninglessness is the depth unfathomed, *Endlessness* the shores of this Ocean. No,

> its shores are deep troughs,
> its depths never sounded!

And the isthmus? That is your "thou-ness." The sea is one, but in your fantastic "thou-ness" it appears as two. Give yourself to these waters and the isthmus of "thou-ness" will vanish as if overflooded and dissolved. The sea of Eternity-without-Beginning will mingle with the waters of Eternity-without-End; the First and the Last will each show itself in the other's hue.

> Today and the day before yesterday,
> yesterday and tomorrow,
> all are one.
> You too: become One!

Then shall you open your eyes and find that everything is you, but that you yourself are lost beyond trace.

> Listen, riffraff:
> Do you want to be ALL?
> Then go,
> go and become NOTHING.

DIVINE FLASHES

FLASH IV

On the fact that in every level
the Beloved—in fact, the lover as well—
is God

Jealous, the Beloved demands that the lover love but Him, need but Him.

> So jealous is He
>   all others are destroyed:
> He must Himself
>   act every part!

Necessarily He makes Himself identical with all things; for the lover, what else is left to love or to need? And no one loves so hugely as He loves Himself. Know now who you are!

> Don't dream this thread
>   is double-ply:
> root and branch
>   are but One.
> Look close: all is He—
>   but He is manifest through *me*.
> All ME, no doubt—
>   but through Him.

The sun shines and a mirror dreams itself the sun. How then should it not begin to love itself? For self-love is in the nature of things. And in truth, the mirror's it-ness is the Sun Itself, since manifestation belongs to It alone: the glass is but a vessel for Its light.

> Love's Sun appeared;
>   I hid myself within it.
> The light you see now
>   is my shining!

It is He who loves Himself in you: What else could it mean to say that "None loves God but God," that "None sees God but God," that

79

DIVINE FLASHES

"None invokes God but God"? Now it is clear, that saying of Mustafa:[7] "O God, give me the joy of my hearing and sight." It is as if he prayed, "Give me enjoyment of Thee, for Thou art my hearing and sight, and *Thou art the best of inheritors* (XXI:89). Thou remainest—and the reality of my hearing and sight remain. But their form will vanish."

> Holy, holy!
> Veils hide His Reality,
> so none but God
> knows who He is.
> Take what you want
> for God is there;
> say what you will about Him
> for He embraces all.

Pardon me this innovation, revealing such secrets. Remember:

> He Himself spoke the Truth
> He Himself listened.
> He Himself showed Himself
> He Himself saw.

Junayd said once, "For thirty years now I've been conversing with God, yet people seem to think I'm talking to *them*!" Through the ears of Moses He heard Himself speak with the flame-tongue of the Bush:

> He speaks
> He listens
> you and I
> but a pretext.

DIVINE FLASHES

FLASH V

On the diversity of the locus-of-manifestation
at every instant, and the disparity of the outward-manifestation
of the Outward in keeping with the
locus-of-manifestation's diversity

In each mirror, each moment the Beloved shows a different face,
a different shape. Each instant reflections change to suit the mirror,
image follows image in harmony with the situation.

> In each mirror, each moment
> a new face reveals His Beauty.
> Now He is Adam, and now
> He appears in the robes of Eve.

Thus He never twice shows the same face; never in two mirrors
does one form appear. Abu Talib al-Makki says, "He never shines
through one shape twice nor manifests as one form in two places."

> His loveliness owns
> a hundred thousand faces;
> gaze upon a different fair one
> in every atom;
> for He needs must show
> to every separate mote
> a different aspect
> of His Beauty.
> "One" is the fountainhead
> of all numbers:
> each split second wells up
> a new perplexity.

Thus it is that every lover gives a different sign of the Beloved
and every gnostic a different explanation; every realized one seems to
point to something different, yet each of them declares,

> "Expressions are many
> but Thy loveliness is one:

DIVINE FLASHES

Each of us refers
 to that single Beauty." (an-Nuri)

"Gazing from every angle
 on that precious countenance
in Thy face we see our own—
 hence the infinitude of descriptions." (Anwari)

To whom do they speak of this Vision? *To him who has a heart* (L:37), to that one whose heart is overcome and transformed by states, one after another, and thus can receive an insight into the Divine transmutations. In his awareness such a one can grasp why Mustafa declared, "He who knows himself knows his Lord" and why Junayd said, "The water's color is the color of the cup." In other words, the form changes every second into another form by reason of the mirror, just as the heart changes with the variegations of its states.

The Prophet tells us that "The heart is like a feather blowing hither and thither in the desert winds"; perhaps the source of these gusts is that breeze to which Mustafa referred when he said, "Do not curse the wind, for it proceeds from the All-merciful's Breath."

If you desire the perfume of this Breath to reach your soul's senses, gaze into the workshop of *Every day He is in a state* (LV:29); then you may justly claim that your own states are reflections of variations in His States and Acts. Then it will be clear to you how the water's color is the cup's color; which is to say that the lover's color is the hue of his Beloved. And you will say,

"The glass grows clear
 the wine grows clear;
one resembles another,
 all is confused
as if there were wine
 and no cup . . .
or cup
 and no wine!" (Sahib ibn 'Abbad)

"My Chinese darling
 I am with you

DIVINE FLASHES

so much that I forget
   am I you or are you me?
No, I am I, you are you . . .
   no . . . I meant you are me . . .
or rather I am I, you are you
   and you are me!"

FLASH VI

On the fact that the lover is the mirror of the
Beloved, and vice versa; each appears in the stage of the other
and is not delimited by its own peculiarities

The end of the affair: The lover sees the Beloved as his own mirror, and himself as the mirror of the Beloved.

Without cease
   gazing into the purity
of the Friend's face, he sees the universe
   imaged in his own reality
and if he once looks back
   into the chamber of his heart
he finds there like a blazing sun
   the sweet face of his heart-thief.

Sometimes one is witness, the other is witnessed; sometimes the
reverse. Sometimes one appears in the other's tints; sometimes one is
perfumed with the other's fragrance.

Love the beautician
   mixes its cosmetics
making Truth into metaphor
   with Its paints;
It sets a trap
   for Mahmud's heart
by combing out the tresses
   of Iyaz.[8]

DIVINE FLASHES

Now Love tailors the lover in a cloak of radiance and perfection, adorning him with the accoutrements of exquisite grace: he looks at himself and sees only the color of the Beloved, sees himself all HIM. He shouts, "Glory be to me, how exalted is my state! Who is like me? Or is there aught but me in the two worlds?" (Bayazid).

Or again, Love drapes the Beloved in the robes of the lover, that the Beloved might climb down from the station of Majesty and Self-sufficiency and plead thus with His lover:

"I swear by My Right
I love you
so to love Me in return
is your responsibility."

Sometimes the Beloved's quest grasps the skirt of the lover, saying, "Is not the desire of the pious drawn out endlessly, their desire to meet Me?" And sometimes the lover's desire raises its head from the neck of the Beloved's cloak[9] and declares, "Verily I desire them more than they desire Me!" (HQ). Sometimes the Beloved Himself becomes the lover's sight, that He might say, "I saw my Lord with the eye of the Lord. I asked 'Who art Thou?' and He answered 'Thou.' " Sometimes the lover becomes the Beloved's voice and says, "*Grant him protection till he hears the words of God*" (IX:6).

In Love alone
can such wonders be.

FLASH VII

On the Self-Manifestation of Love
through Its Nondelimitation in all the loci-of-manifestation
and Its appearance in the clothing of Belovedness
for all kinds of perception and cognition

Love courses through all things.... No, It *is* all things. How deny It when nothing else exists? What has appeared—if not for Love—would not have been. All has appeared from Love, through Love, and Love courses through it.... No, all of it is Love.

DIVINE FLASHES

Love is the lover's essence, nor could this essence cease to be, however his attachment may flit from beloved to beloved.

> Shift, transfer your heart where you will—
> Love belongs but to the First Beloved.

Love where you may, you will have loved Him; turn your face whatever way, it turns toward Him—even if you know it not.

> Everyone drawn to a beloved
> must be subject to him.
> All are subject to Thee
> but know it not.

The poet means to say,

> Whether they know Thee or not
> all creatures of the world
> now and forever-without-end
> bend but toward Thee.
> All love for someone else
> is but a whiff
> of Thy perfume:
> none else can be loved.

It is not so much wrong as impossible to love other than Him, for whatever we love (aside from that love which springs from the very essence of the lover, the cause of which is unknown), we love either for its beauty, or its goodness—and both of these belong to Him alone.

> The beauty of each lovely boy
> each comely girl
> derives from His—
> on loan.

But beauty and goodness alike are hidden behind the veils of intermediate causes, behind the faces of those we love. Majnun may gaze at Layla's beauty, but this Layla is only a mirror. Therefore the Prophet said, "Whoso has loved, remained chaste, kept the secret and died, dies a martyr." Majnun's contemplation of her loveliness is aimed at a beauty beside which all else is ugliness. He may not know that "God is beautiful" (H)—but who else is worthy of possessing beauty?

> That which owns
> no existence in itself—
> from whence would it derive
> such beauty?

And also, "God loves beauty,"[10] for beauty by its very nature is made to be loved. God with Majnun's eye looks upon His own beauty in Layla, and through Majnun He loves Himself.

> He who is equal to Your love[11]
> is You Yourself
> for You and You alone
> gaze forever at Your beauty.

Let no censorious pen scratch out the name of a Majnun who views in the mirror of his loved one the Absolute Beauty Itself.

> A lover like that
> whose story we've heard
> is not to be found in every place
> the sun may shine.

No indeed! the very idea!

> Let no son of Adam
> prattle to you of an "absolute love"
> for there in the city of "love unqualified"
> what business has mere man?

All that exists is the mirror of His Beauty; so everything is beautiful, and He loves everything. Or to be precise, He loves Himself. In fact, any lover you see loves only himself, for seeing but his own face in the mirror of his beloved, he must needs come to self-amorousness. The Prophet said, "The believer is the mirror of the believer"—and God is the "Believer."

DIVINE FLASHES

Grasp this vision:
    look closely and behold
in every atom of the universe
    a world-displaying cup.[12]

A lover sees his beloved's image in the mirror of his own essence—but no, it is the Beloved Himself seeing Himself. After all, the lover sees with eyes, and the Tradition says, "I—God—become his ears, his eyes, his hand and his tongue" (HQ). So the lover's eyes *are* the Beloved, and all he sees, knows, says and hears is the Beloved Himself; for "verily we are in Him and belong to Him." In terms of manifestation therefore lover and Beloved, seeker and Sought, are one. But not everyone can grasp this. No,

How can a beggar
    become a sultan?
Bah! How can a fly
    become Solomon?

How can this beggar
    become the sultan
when he already
    is the sultan?

Bizarre, bizarre
    and rare indeed!
Since one is the same as the other
how can *this* become *that*?

FLASH VIII

On an allusion to the theophanies
which occur for the wayfarers and the properties
of these theophanies

The Beloved shows His face in either the looking-glass of form or the mirror of meaning—or beyond both form and meaning. If He displays His Beauty to the lover's gaze in the garment of *form*, the lover joys in witnessing and takes nourishment from the sight. Then the mysterious Tradition "I saw my Lord in the loveliest form" will uncover for him the significance of the Verse *Wherever you turn, there is the Face of God* (II:115); and *God is the light of the heavens and earth* (XXIV:35) will explain for him the lover's plea:

> Come inhabit my eyes
> and gaze on Him.

Then he will know how

> all the world's lows
> and highs are You:
> I know not what You are
> but You are everything.

And he will understand why the poet said

> I have a friend
> whose form is body and soul
> —but which body, what soul?
> The Universe is His form;
> every fair meaning,
> every fair form
> I gaze upon—
> that is His form.

But if His Majesty rides forth to attack from behind the veil of *meaning* in the World of Spirits, He will kidnap the lover away from himself so totally that neither name nor clue will survive. The lover will then find no enjoyment of witnessing nor even a taste of discovery. Here the annihilation of "him who was not" and the subsistence of "Him Who always was" reveal to the lover how

> You appear to the one
> who receives from You
> subsistence after annihilation;
> he lacks all temporal being
> since You
> are he.

DIVINE FLASHES

Now, if the Beloved should cast aside the veils of both *form* and *meaning* from His Beauty and Majesty, then would the Overdominance of the Essence proclaim to the lover,

> "Let there be in this city
> but you ... or ME
> for no government can survive
> a double kingship!"

So ... begone! for "When God's river overflows, Jesus River disappears."[13]

Once a gnat appeared at the Court of Solomon to bring suit against the Wind. Solomon ordered him, "Bring this enemy of yours to me." The gnat retorted, "If I had the strength to compel him I should never have come to you to complain in the first place!"

> What mirror can He fit?
> When does He ever show us His Face?

FLASH IX

On that which the Beloved and the lover
each contemplates in the mirror of the other, the levels
of the lover's direct-vision and its final end

So the Beloved is the mirror of the lover, and in Him the lover sees with his own eyes but himself. And the lover is the mirror of the Beloved, in which He sees His Names and Attributes and the manifestation of His Divine properties. Now when the lover discovers that the Names and Attributes of the Beloved are identical with the Divine Self, he must exclaim,

> "You witnessed Yourself in me,
> that Self which is one in Essence
> but multiple in its mastery
> of Attributes and Names.

DIVINE FLASHES

> I witnessed in You
>   a reality which transcends
> my multiplicity, and through which
>   seer and seen are united.
>
> My world-displaying cup
>   is Your joy-augmenting face
> but Your world-displaying cup
>   is my reality."[14]

Sometimes this is the mirror of that, sometimes that of this. If the lover peers into the Beloved's glass and sees there his own inwardness and meaning, shaped in the mold of his own outward form, then he has seen merely his own self with his own eye. But if he beholds some corporeal form, in a shape other than his own, and realizes that beyond it lies Something Else, then he has beheld the form of the Beloved with the Beloved's eye.

Then again it may happen that the lover himself is a mirror gazing at itself, and since the form of the Beloved which appears therein is determined by the shape of the mirror, then we may say that Domination belongs to the lover-as-mirror, since "The water's color is the cup's color." And if he sees this form as other than his own shape, he will know it to be that "Giver of Forms" Who embraces all forms: *And God embraces them on all sides* (LXXXV:20).

When the sincere lover stamps his foot upon the neck of the world of forms, we know his Spiritual Resolve desires only a Beloved of transcendent attributes; and that he will not submit his own neck to any beloved chained with the fetters of shape and image, nor the tie of knowledge and union. No, all forms are now erased from his contemplation: he sees the Beloved directly, without the intermediary aid of form. As the Sufis say, "God can be seen clearly only when formal limitations dissolve."

> How can Meaning be squeezed
>   into the box of Form?
> What business has the sultan
>   in this beggar's realm?

DIVINE FLASHES

In the end, what can he know
    who worships form, heedless of Meaning?
Tell me: what business can he have
    with the beauty of a hidden Beloved?

FLASH X

On what becomes joined to that which is Outward
in the locus-of-manifestation in respect of the locus, and
what occurs to the locus in respect of the outward-manifestation
of the Outward within it

Manifestation, ceaseless and perpetual, is the Beloved's attribute; concealment—hiddenness—that of the lover. When the Beloved's form appears in the lover's mirror-entity, that glass—in keeping with its own realities—exercises a certain influence on the image which is manifested, just as manifestation itself bestows a name on what appears.

Amazing! My mother
    gave birth to her own father!

Here I-ness and we-ness appear, you-ness and he-ness are manifest.

When the lover contemplates the Beloved's beauty in form's mirror, pain and pleasure are born, grief and joy are manifest, fear and hope come together, contraction and expansion make their rounds. But when he strips off the robes of form and dives into Unity's All-embracing Ocean, he knows nothing of torment or bliss, expectation or dread, fear or hope; for these depend on past and future, and he now drowns in a sea where Time is abolished, where all is Now upon Now.

Wander in salt deserts:
    you are lost.
And is this roaring sea
    less than salt? ('Attar)

91

DIVINE FLASHES

You fear either the veil or the lifting of the veil; but here you are safe from both: for a veil cannot be imagined save between two things, and here there can be but one. Here there can be no fear of the unveiling, which terrifies only him who dreads burning in Splendor's radiance;

> but how can he who is flame
> be eaten by fire?

> One are Kaaba and synagogue
> for the nonexistent,
> and for the shadow, heaven
> and hell are one.

> When dawn rides forth
> in the Wine-star's light
> then equal at last
> are the sober and the drunk.

LIGHT will not burn light, for the lesser radiance is sucked into the greater and absorbed. Unity's People neither fear nor hope, know neither bliss nor torment. Someone asked Bayazid, "How did you pass the morning?" and he replied, "For me, no morning, no evening."

> Here where I am
> is no dawn or dusk
> no dread or expectation
> state or station.

"Morning and evening pertain to him only who is limited by attributes, but I . . . I have no attributes.

> Indeed, how should I have attributes
> when I have no essence?"

DIVINE FLASHES

FLASH XI

*On the rejection of a number of false ideas
which face the wayfarers to God, through which they fall into the abyss of
incarnationism, unification, atheism, and heresy*

Know that between form and the mirror no true unification, no "incarnation," can exist.

> What a meddlesome bore,
> the one who here confuses
> theophany
> and "incarnation"! (Sana'i)

Unification and incarnation could take place between two essences, but to contemplation's eye there exists in all existence but one Object of contemplation.

> Reality is one,
> properties differ:
> a secret revealed
> to gnostics alone.

He who has lifted the veil sees multiplicity in properties, not in the Essence; hence he knows that changes in properties cannot touch Essence, which owns a perfection subject to no mutability. Light merely seems to change as it shines through colored glass, but

> light has no color.
> Its rays shine through the glass
> and only then
> do hues and tints appear.

Don't you understand?

> Come then into my eyes
> and . . . look!

and you will see

DIVINE FLASHES

a sun shining
    through a thousand bits of glass
beaming to plain sight through each
    a ray of color.
Why should any difference appear
    between this one and that?
All light is one
    but colors a thousandfold.

FLASH XII

On the arrival of the wayfarers at the end
of the Journey to God and the beginning of the Journey in God,
and on the nature of the latter

When this door is opened, truly opened, we shall retreat into the
cell of our nonexistence and behold ourselves and our Beloved in the
mirror of each-otherness. We shall travel no further, for "After the
conquest of Mecca, why emigrate to Medina?"

        This mirror of form
            has no need of wayfaring
        for it receives its form
            from Light.

Indeed, no one ever really leaves this cell, *so where are you going?*
(LXXXI:26).

        I shall not leave
            this luminous house
        nor ever depart
            from this blessed city.

Exiled from here? Impossible! The Prophet said, "In my community,
no traveling."[15] Here the road ends, aspiration finds rest and agitation calm, the climb is over, all attributes peel away, all allusions ex-
plode, and the tyranny of "from" and "to" is overthrown; for how

can Being take sides when it knows no beginning, no end? The tongue of seclusion here recites,

> "I sought solitude
> with my loved one
> yet find there is no one here
> but myself.
> And if there were
> 'someone else'
> I should not in truth
> have attained her."

If there should be journeying after this, it must be *in* Him and *in* His Attributes. Once Bayazid heard someone recite this verse: *On the day We gather the godfearing to the All-merciful in groups* (XIX:85). He cried out, "But those who are already with Him, where shall *they* be gathered?"

Someone overheard him and said, "From the Name 'All-compeller' to the Name 'All-merciful,' from the Name 'All-subjugator' to the Name 'All-compassionate!' "

FLASH XIII

On the luminous and tenebrous veils
which render the Journey necessary, the Journey which is
to remove those veils

The Beloved hid His Face with seventy thousand veils of light and darkness, that the lover might grow used to seeing Him behind the screen of creation. But when at last the sight is accustomed to this trick, and Love rattles the chains of ardor, then one by one—with Love's succor and the strength of desire—the lover may tear away those veils. The splendrous rays of Majesty will sear away all fantasies of otherness, till the lover sits upon Love's very throne. He will become ALL; and

95

DIVINE FLASHES

> what he takes he'll take
> with His hand from Him,
> what he gives he'll give
> from Him to Him.

Perhaps the Prophet was alluding to this when he said, "The prayer *without you* is better than seventy." That is, a prayer offered without your you-ness excels seventy ordinary ones; for while you remain with yourself, all seventy thousand veils hang before you. But when you are absent from yourself, who remains to be veiled?

Some say that these veils are man's attributes, the luminous ones such as knowledge, certainty, states and stations and all virtues; and the tenebrous such as ignorance, doubt, custom and habit and all vice.

> They say the veils of light and dark
> lie in certainty and doubt
> and the like. But this
> is the measure of their incapacity!

Mark well: if these veils were merely human attributes, they would be burnt to nothing; for as the Prophet said, "If God were to remove them, the Splendor of His Face would incinerate the eyes of all creatures who gazed at Him." That is: If creaturely attributes were exposed to this unadulterated light, they would be utterly consumed. But in fact this never happens; vision never burns them, nor do they cease to block our sight.

So these veils must not be human but Divine, God's Names and Attributes: luminous ones such as manifestation, benevolence, and Beauty; tenebrous ones such as nonmanifestation, all-subjugation, and Majesty. These Names and Attributes must not be raised, for if they were, the Unity of the Essence would blaze forth from behind the screen of Might, and all things would be totally annihilated. For it may happen that through the Names and Attributes all things become qualified by all-pervading Existence, even though these things actually come into being through the theophany of the Essence. But the theophany of the Essence itself acts from behind the veil of Attributes and Names.

DIVINE FLASHES

So: His veils are His own Names and Attributes. As the author of *Hearts' Food*[16] puts it, "Essence is veiled by Attributes, Attributes by Acts."[17] Ultimately He Himself is His own veil, for He is hidden by the very intensity of His manifestation and occulted by the very potency of His Light.

> You are Inward, not appearing
>   to those with eyes to see
> for how can He be seen Who is hid
>   by His own Reality?

We see, but know not what we see: and must say,

> Everywhere veiled
>   by Your own Face
> You are hidden from the world
>   in Your very manifestation.
> Look where I will
>   I see Your Face alone;
> in all these idols
>   I see only You.
> Jealous lest You be recognized
>   at every instant
> You dress Your Beauty
>   in a different cloak.

How could anything else veil Him? for veils belong only to the limited, and He has no limits. All you behold in the world of form and meaning is His Form—but He is unbound by any form. Where He is not, nothing exists—but wherever He is . . . that thing is also naught.

> You are the world—
>   but how can You be seen?
> Are You not the soul as well?
>   Yet how can You be hidden?
> How can You be manifest?
>   for You are occult always.
> Yet how can You be hidden
>   when You are eternally seen?

DIVINE FLASHES

Hidden, manifest,
    both at once:
You are *not this, not that—*
    yet both at once.

FLASH XIV

On the differentiation between the Bow
of Necessary-Being and the Bow of Possible-Existence,
the Station of Two Bows' Length *and its mystery and inward,*
which is the Station of Or Nearer, *and on*
the differentiation between the two

Imagine lover and Beloved as a single circle divided by a line into two bow-shaped arcs. This line but seems to exist, yet does not, and if it be erased at the moment of the Meeting, the circle will appear again as one—as in fact it really is. This then is the secret of *Two Bows' Length.*

The world but seems to be
    yet is nothing more
than a line drawn
    between light and shadow.
Decipher the message
    of this dream-script
and learn to distinguish time
    from Eternity.

Break the code of this line and know beyond doubt that

All is nothing,
    nothing.
All is He,
    all is HE.

But wait! Even if the line is erased, the circle will still not appear as it did at first. The line's effect will not altogether vanish: It will be gone, but its trace will remain.

DIVINE FLASHES

Make no mistake:
>he who is lost
in God
>is not God Himself.

His Absolute Uniqueness cannot permit any one-ness born of the unification-of-two to lurk about the precincts of the Pavilion of Unity.

>After this,
>>something else . . .
>something subtle.
>>In His eyes
>it is better
>>to conceal it,
>more graceful
>>to hide it away.

Unity in respect to the Names may be called "Unity of Multiplicity" and in respect to the Essence "Unity of Entity." Both are referred to by the same word: *unus*, one. The One threads through all things, as does the number one through all numerals: If "one" did not exist, the numerals would not exist, could not be named. Or if "one" were to appear in its own name, the realities of the other numbers could never appear.

>If You are Everything
>>then who are all these people?
>And if I am nothing
>>what's all this noise about?
>You are Totality,
>>everything is You. Agreed.
>Then that which is "other-than-You"—
>>*what is it?*
>Oh, indeed I know:
>>Nothing exists but You;
>but tell me:
>>Whence this confusion?

Reader, you may grasp His Oneness through your own oneness. Listen: you are one, and can come to know that One only through this one. Simple: One comes to know "Oneself." *You* and *it* are not involved in the slightest.

The Profession of Unity is explained by this formula, though few indeed realize it: "Any individual number multiplied by oneness results in one individual number."

$$1 \times 1 = 1$$

FLASH XV

On the lover's actions
and the nature of the ascription of all things to him,
and on felicity and wretchedness

The lover is the Beloved's shadow, and follows wherever He goes:

> When will shadow
> ever be cloven from light?

Thus following, he cannot go astray. *Surely my Lord is on a straight path* (XI:56), and since the lover's forelock is in the Lord's hand, there is but one way to go. *There is no creature that crawls but He takes it by the forelock* (XI:56).

> Vanity? There is no vanity!
> Creatures were not made
> for aimlessness, even if their acts
> do not always hit the mark.
> These acts flow according
> to the molds of the Names,
> and the Wisdom
> of the Attributes
> drives them at last
> to the Divine Decree. (Ibn al-Farid)

DIVINE FLASHES

They asked Junayd, "What is the Profession of Unity?" and he replied, "I heard a minstrel chant,

> 'They sang me my heart's desire;
> I sang what they sang.
> I was where they were,
> and they were where I am.'"

They asked al-Hallaj, "To which religious School do you belong?" and he answered, "God's own."

> He who limned
> a thousand worlds with paint—
> you layabout!—do you expect
> He'll use your color or mine?
> Our paints and tints
> are but opinion and fantasy.
> He is colorless
> and we must adopt His hue.

Look: a shadow lies crooked upon the ground because the very earth is laid rough; but no, that crookedness is straightness itself, for the perfection, the "straightness" of the eyebrow is in its sinuous curve.

> Only because it is bent
> is this piece of wood a bow.

Reality is a sphere: wherever you place your finger, there is its dead center.

But I digress. Know then, that when Love's sun shines from the orient of the Unseen, the Beloved pitches the tent of His Shadow in the desert of manifestation. He addresses the lover:

> "Now then, won't you
> behold My shadow?

Hast thou not regarded thy Lord, how He stretched out the shadow? (XXV:45). Do you not see Me in the waxing of this dark silhouette?"

DIVINE FLASHES

For in this house, everything
has the look of its landlord.

Say: Everything acts according to His manner (XVII:84); don't you see
that if the object is immobile, its shadow cannot move? *Had He willed,
He would have made the shadow still* (XXV:45). Indeed, if Unity's Sun
shone from the dawn of Might no wisp of shadow would survive, for
a shade which dares live near the sun is embraced: *Thereafter We seize
it to Ourselves, drawing it gently* (XXV:46).

Ah, the desert
is drowned in sun;
no shadow could venture here
for even a second.

What a marvel! When the sun shines, the shadow vanishes—but
without sun, no shadow at all! Each thing has an essence, and the
shadow's essence is the object which casts it. As this object moves, so
moves the shadow.

While the hand moves
the shadow must follow.
Since the shadow gains its substance
from the hand
it has none of itself.
That which derives existence
from something else
how can we say
it truly exists?
It has a name, yes,
but is not that existence
which subsists through God.

The Shaykh al-Islam Abdullah Ansari says, "Where a created being derives subsistence from an uncreated, the former is annihilated
in the latter. When the servant's reality is truly pure, his I-ness is but
a borrowing. And what is I-ness? It consists only of words: 'I' and
'thou.' If you really exist, where is God? And if God exists, God is
one, not two."

102

DIVINE FLASHES

"I" and "you"
  have made of man a two-ness.
Without these words, you are I
  and I am you.

FLASH XVI

*On an example through which it becomes clear
that the many-ness of diverse shapes has no effect upon the Oneness
of the True One, so that It remains in Its True Oneness
in the very midst of many-ness*

The shadow-play master behind the screen performs his contra-
dictory mummery, his diverse turns and steps, jugglery and props, all
him, and hid behind the scrim. When they strike the set you'll know
these shapes and their posturings for what they really are:

> the whole show but one
>   lone puppeteer
> hid behind his
>   screen of art.
> He tears it away
>   reveals himself alone
> and all illusions
>   vanish into nothing. (Ibn al-Farid)

The secret of *Surely thy Lord is wide in forgiveness* (LIII:32): All
creatures are His "covering" or curtain.[18]

> His presence is a sun
>   and heaven and earth
> I find are but
>   a parasol . . .

. . . and He is the Agent behind that sun-shade. But *They perceive not*
(VII:95). Only if the secret of *God created you and what you do*

DIVINE FLASHES

(XXXVII:96) were to wink its eye at them, would they ever come to know perforce that

> All power, all activity is ours
> only so much as HE is us.

Only then would they ask: How should that which is nonexistence in itself act, or have power?

> Know that the soul's prostration
> is also from Him
> and that the cloud is generous
> because of the sun.

The source of activity is one, but everywhere displays new colors and is called by a different name. *Watered with one water, and some of them We prefer in produce above others* (XIII:4).

FLASH XVII

*On the variegation of the theophanies of the Beloved
and the advance of the lover in preparedness in keeping with
these theophanies; on the words which this group
has uttered concerning the meaning of "preparedness";
and on an allusion to the never-endingness
of the Way in the Journey to God*

Each moment from each of the myriad windows of the Attributes the Beloved shows the lover a different face, and from these rays of light the lover's inner eye gains illumination with each flash, fresh vision with each passing instant. The more beauty is displayed, the more overpowering the love; the more overpowering the love, the more beauty is displayed . . . and all the while the gap grows wider between Beloved and lover. Finally the lover flees the Loved-one's cruelty, flies to the Refuge of Love Itself, and clings to Oneness that he may escape duality.

DIVINE FLASHES

The Manifestation of Lights, so it has been said, extends as far as the preparedness, and the Effusion of Gnosis as far as the receptivity.

> No fault of the sun if the owl
> gains nothing from its light.
> The more you purify the face of your heart
> the better prepared for theophany. (Sana'i)

True enough . . . but "O Thou who makest blessings to appear before they are deserved!" That is, when the Beloved would display Himself in the lover's mystic eye, He lends that organ a glimmer of His own Beauty-ray. With this light the lover can see and take pleasure in that Divine loveliness.

After the lover has enjoyed through that light his share of contemplation, again the radiance of the Beloved's Face bestows upon his eye a brighter light—with which yet greater lights can be perceived. And so and so it goes, like a thirsty man gulping saltwater: The more he drinks, the more rages his thirst. The more you acquire, the more you aspire.

> The more I gaze
> at Your face, the more
> my eyes incline
> toward Your vision
> like one who dies of thirst
> by the ocean shore,
> lips to the wave,
> thirstier and thirstier.

> Seek not, find not—
> except in this one case:
> Until you find the Friend
> you'll never seek Him.

One who thirsts for *this* water can never be satisfied.

DIVINE FLASHES

He cannot glance away
    without glancing back,
his desire
    rekindled.

Once Yahya Ma'adh Razi wrote to Bayazid:

"So drunk am I
    from His love-wine
another drop
    would finish me!"

Bayazid wrote back:

"Cup after cup
    of love I drink
but neither wine nor vision
    ever seems to run dry!"

I could see You a thousand times a day
and still desire to see You once again.

A saint once declared, "Between me and my Lord the only difference is that I come forward in servitude." That is, my poverty and my preparedness are the key to His Generosity.

Someone heard him and protested, "Who was it then prepared you first?" Indeed, what is the key to this *primary* Generosity? for *with Him are the Keys of the Unseen* (VI:59).[19]

When Kharaqani reached this point he cried out, "I am less than my Lord by two years!"[20]

Abu Talib al-Makki remarked, "Kharaqani spoke the truth, for God creates nonexistence just as He creates existence."[21]

Someone else said, "The Divine Will has no effect upon the preparedness, for the reality of the preparedness never changes. Rather, the Will singles out a specific locus to receive a specific preparedness." In other words, God in the World of the Unseen makes manifest the effects of a nonmanifest theophany within the reality of the servant. This takes the form of a principial preparedness by means of which the theophany of entified existence may be received. When this theophany is actualized, the servant acquires through it a further preparedness in the Visible World, which permits him to become a receptacle for the theophany of mystical vision within external existence. Finally, in keeping with his states, a new preparedness is actualized at every moment, thus opening for him the door of infinite theophanies. And since these theophanies are endless, each bringing in its wake a particular knowledge, the servant's knowledge likewise has no end. Thus *Say: My Lord, increase me in knowledge!* (XX:114).

Those whose thirst is quenched imagine that since they have attained Union they have reached the goal and are joined with the object of their desire. They rest content with *Unto Him you shall be returned* (II:28). But beware! beware, for till eternity the way-stations of Union's Path are never out-traveled. No one returns whence he started, so how could wayfaring find its end or the road reach a final destination? If the place of Return were the same as the place of Origin, what good would it be to set out or arrive?

Abu-l-Hasan an-Nuri describes the length and endlessness of the Path:

> I contemplated—but never
>   contemplated a vision I had seen.
> The vision of a sweetheart-never-witnessed:
>   how precious!

Yearning should spur even those who have attained Union to aspire higher and higher still. Otherwise they are defined by what they have found and stay stuck in the station of inadequacy: "Then they send them back to the palaces"[22] ... *therein to dwell forever, desiring no removal out of them* (XVIII:108).

DIVINE FLASHES

FLASH XVIII

On the reason for
the lover's movement and seeking and his advance
forever and ever

The lover once drowsed at peace with existence and nonexistence, and had not yet seen the Beloved's face. Suddenly the music of the word *BE!* woke him from the sleep of nothingness; that note rapt him in ecstasy and whirled him into being. How it went to his head, the taste of that melody!

> Love set a bonfire
> in his very soul!

> Often Love conquers the ear
> before the eye.

Love overwhelmed him and transformed that peacefulness—inner and outer—to a wild dance of the Spirit, set to this tune:

> Truly the constant pilgrim:
> the lover to the one he loves.

This music will never fade nor the dance wind down till the end of Eternity, for what we desire is Infinite. The lover whispers,

> "As I opened my eyes
> I saw your face;
> I heard your voice
> as I listened."

So he is caught in this ceaseless and invisible dance, our lover, though to look at him you would think him calm enough. *You shall see the mountains, that you supposed fixed, passing by like clouds* (XXVII:88). How could he sit still when every atom of the universe prods him to move? each atom a word, each word a Name, each Name with a tongue, each tongue speaking ... and the lover with an ear for every utterance. Listen closely: the speaker and hearer are one, for "audition is a bird which flies from God to God."

Junayd chided Shibli: "The secrets we hide in the cellars you boom from the pulpit!" Shibli replied, "I speak, I listen. Who else exists in heaven and earth?"

These perfumes:
  musk, clove . . .
all from the hyacinthine shadows
  of those tresses.
You think you hear
  a nightingale's song . . .
No. It is the voice
  of the Rose.

FLASH XIX

On the scope of the lover's capacity
and the perfect all-embracingness and completeness of his receptivity,
and on the meaning of "Heart" and
"True Oneness"

Purified of all entifications, the lover's heart is like that landscape where the domes of Might fill the horizon, that place where the seas of the Seen and the Unseen flow together. Such a heart possesses a Spiritual-Resolve

which could gulp
  from the flagon of the sea
a thousand draughts of wine
  and still beg one more.

So vast is this heart that earth cannot contain it, and all the worlds might vanish in its embrace. God hoists the tent of Unity in the courtyard of Oneness. There He holds a sultan's levee, there He sees to this and that affair; and makes manifest tying and untying, contraction and expansion, inconstancy and constancy.

DIVINE FLASHES

Contraction:
 He hides what He revealed.
Expansion:
 He gives back what He concealed.

An idol so exquisite
 the world cannot hold it:
how, how does it make its home
 in my narrow heart?

Bayazid describes his own heart's wide circle: "If the Divine Throne and all it compasses were to pass through a corner of the gnostic's heart, he would not even know it."

Junayd adds: "How indeed could he know it? For when the temporal is placed next to the Eternal, no trace of it remains." When our Bayazid contemplates such a heart, unstained by temporality, he sees nothing but the Eternal. How could he not cry out "Glory to me!"?

A man filled with water a pitcher made of ice. The sun blazed upon it, and jug and water were one. "In the two worlds," he exclaimed, "nothing stirs but HE!"

Hunter and prey
 and bait in the trap
candle, candlestick
 flame and moth
Beloved and lover
 soul and soul's desire
saki, fellow drinkers
 wine and cup: all
HE.

How wonderful! "The heart of My servant encompasses Me" (HQ) and "The heart is between the two fingers of the All-merciful" (H). He is within the heart, but the heart is within His grasp. This must be what the poet meant when he wrote

My heart is tangled in your locks
 but you

DIVINE FLASHES

live in the center
    of my sorrowing heart.
But my darling, you should know
    that because of your subtle grace
you yourself are held and locked
    in the chains of your tresses.

Bound in His own fetters, He cares nothing for "others," and fits only within Himself. Singleness rests in Singleness alone, Unity finds peace but in Oneness. This is the heart's reality—but how few come to know it!

One heart-realized sage described his secret whisperings and gave news of the quality and measure of his "moment":[23]

"Whose beloved are You?"
    I asked,
"You who are so
    unbearably beautiful?"
"My own," He replied,
    "for I am one and alone
love, lover, and beloved
    mirror, beauty, eye."

FLASH XX

On the division of the Attributes
into "ontological" and "nonexistential," and the attribution
of the ontological Attributes to the Beloved and the nonexistential
Attributes to the lover; on the meaning of "poverty"
and the explication of its levels; and on
"Poverty is blackness of face in the two worlds"
and the superiority of poverty
over riches

Upon the Beloved Love bestows dominance and independence; upon the lover meekness and need. Thus it is from Love and not from the Beloved's Might that the lover suffers, for it often happens that the Beloved Himself is a slave—"O my slaves, I derive from you."[24] But in any case, the Beloved's attribute is wealth, that of the lover poverty. This poor man "needs everything, but nothing needs him!"

Why is he so needy? The true lover gazes toward the reality of things:

> My eyes so fix
> upon your image
> that whatever I gaze at
> I imagine you.

Wherever he looks he finds that Face and therefore needs everything he sees. "Poverty is intrinsic need; it has nothing to do with this or that."

And why does nothing need the lover? One can only need something which exists. But the lover, outwardly detached and inwardly disengaged, has returned the robe of existence and all its trappings—which he only held in trust—to the Beloved. *God commands you to deliver trusts back to their owners* (IV:58). Again he has donned the patched cloak of his own nothingness. "He is with God as he was in Eternity-without-beginning,"[25] and in such a state, who needs him?

But ... in poverty there comes a state wherein the poor man himself needs nothing. As one of them said, "The poor man is not in need of God Himself!" Need, after all, is an attribute of the existent; but he who dives into the sea of nothingness needs no more. His poverty is complete. "When his poverty is complete, he is God." And what does God need? Nothing whatsoever.

> You are nothing
> when you wed the One;
> but you are everything
> when you become nothing.

Such a man, needless of God, is obviously higher than the lover we began with. For the lover, still in need of all things, sees the Desired One only behind the veil of all things. But as for the one who perfects the Retreat of being and nonbeing, existence and nonexistence, Junayd says of him: "The poor man needs neither himself nor his Lord"; and Shaykh 'Ali al-Jurayri: "For me the poor man has neither heart nor Lord." He has left existence behind for nonexistence. If he were to use his own eye to gaze on the Friend he would see nothing but the dark reflection of his own nothingness, merely himself veiled with the veil of "Poverty is blackness of face in the two houses" (H). No light will he find in the house of existence to whiten his visage, nothing manifest in the house of nonexistence with which he might sponge off his blackface. "Poverty is near to unbelief" (H).

> In our religion
> the "Greatest Blackness"
> is to wear
> the weeds of poverty.[26]

Know that the rich man for the most part is far in the extremity of nearness, while the poor man is always near in the extremity of farness.

> Love's wind storms and rips to shreds
> the brother of wealth
> but let it waft over poverty and see
> how the breezes will nourish it.

What does this mean? Suppose a millionaire and a pauper set out together for the Land of Love. A bright lamp burns in the rich man's hand, his companion holds but a smouldering stick. Suddenly a breeze springs up from that realm, and—puff!—the millionaire's lamp is blown out; but the poor man's meager torch flares up and crackles. "I am with those whose hearts are rent and whose graves are obliterated" (HQ); now, is that not a fine polo mallet

> with which the broken ones
> may win the ball from the field?

DIVINE FLASHES

FLASH XXI

*On the fact that the lover
must be cleansed of individual motives, eliminate his own seeking
and will, and gaze upon the Desire of the Beloved;
but that he must distinguish between the approved
and the disapproved*

The lover must keep company with the Beloved devoid of all motive; he must wipe out all desires, deliver himself to the Beloved's want, and abandon all ambition, for aspiration only blocks his path. What you get by wanting is only as big as your capacity for desire. Give up desire therefore, think that whatever you get is what you want, and in this acceptance find ease and joy.

> Renounce desire
>   a hundred times
> or else not once
>   will you embrace your Desire.

Only if what happens is disapproved should you strive against it and change it as much as you can. This striving may perhaps bring about some change which the Beloved approves. If the lover has been unveiled to the extent that he can see the Friend's face direct in every form, nevertheless he must disapprove the disapproved, even if he sees that face in it. The face the Friend turns toward the disapproved is one of disapproval; for *He does not approve unbelief for His servants* (XXXIX:7). The lover who experiences God through God and sees the whole world as God must reject all blameworthiness through God, in God, and for God, with his argument sustained by God. In that which is prohibited by Divine Law he will not perceive God's Beauty, and will therefore avoid it. In fact by his very nature he will not feel the slightest desire for it.

But here some obscurity obtrudes. He is under the sway of theophany, and theophany embraces all things. How then can he banish theophany from his own gaze? The answer: Theophany is of two sorts, that of the Essence, and that of the Names and Attributes. The former cannot be repelled, but in the latter case one can reject wrathful theophany by means of benevolent theophany. In all which offends Divine Law he must see the signs of Wrath and Majesty; in all which is approved, the signs of Benevolence and Beauty. Here he must say, "I take refuge in Thy approval from Thy anger!" (H). But faced with the theophany of the Essence he may say, "I take refuge in Thee from Thee!" (H).

> What shall I do
> if not fly from Thee to Thee?
> To whom shall I go,
> to whom recite my tale?

FLASH XXII

*On the mystery of the command
given to the wayfaring lover that he must occupy himself with the forms
of acts and works, that is, formal and supraformal ascetic practices,
and on the fact that he becomes veiled by them from the
direct vision of the All-comprehensive Entity
—a mystery which is the distance desired
by the Beloved; and on the meaning of proximity in the very midst
of distance, which is the result of
this command*

The lover's duty: to like what the Friend approves, even if it be nothing but remoteness and separation. And in fact, this is usually the case, for He wants us to seek refuge from His cruelty in Love; "Hellfire is a whip to drive God's people to God" (H) perhaps alludes to something of this sort. The lover must like his own exile and submit to separation, finding his habit in this line:

> I want Union with Him
> He wants separation for me—
> so I abandon my desire
> to His.

He likes separation not in itself but only because the Beloved likes it.

DIVINE FLASHES

All the Beloved does
is lovable.

So what can the poor lover do? What can he say except,

"Searching for separation
yearning for Union
I am free of both:
Thy love suffices."

Or, rather, he must savor separation more than Union, enjoy remoteness better than nearness—if he knows the Friend desires it. In fact, remoteness has a greater intimacy than nearness, and separation more than Union. After all, in nearness and Union the lover is merely qualified by his own desires, while in exile and separation he is qualified by the will of the Beloved.

A thousand times
sweeter than Union
I find this separation
You have desired.

In Union
I am the servant of self,
in separation
my Master's slave;
and I would rather
be busy with the Friend
whatever the situation
than with myself.

If a lover who is qualified by the Beloved's attributes likes remoteness, he will thereby have loved the Beloved. The extreme reach of Union is found in the very exile of remoteness—but how few understand!

Know then that the cause of the lover's remoteness is his own attributes—but that these attributes *are* the Beloved Himself. Say "I seek refuge from Thee in Thee" (H) and understand that

DIVINE FLASHES

When I clutched at His skirt
I found His hand in my sleeve.[27]

How can this be? Recite this Tradition and you will see what I mean:
"I do not praise Thee, Thou art as Thou praise Thyself."[28]

FLASH XXIII

On the perfection
of the lover's disengaging the soul and his all-aloneness;
on his becoming cut off from all things,
even the Beloved; and on the Inherent Oneness
of Love

Love's fire falls into the heart and consumes all it finds, erasing from the heart even the image of the Beloved. Surely Majnun burned in such a conflagration when they told him, "Layla has arrived!" for he then replied, "I myself am Layla," and hooded himself in the robe of detachment.

Layla pleaded, "Lift up your head. It is I, your beloved.

Look, see who it is
from whom you remain so distant."

He answered,

"Go from me.
Your love
has stolen away my mind
from you yourself.

Once I was happy to see you
but now
I have lost interest
in anything but Love."

DIVINE FLASHES

Mustafa revealed the essence of this station in his prayer, "O God, make Thy Love more dear to me than even my eyes and ears." It is as if he had said, "O Thou Who art my very sight and hearing,

> occupy me so
> > with Thy Love
> > that in such Love I no more
> > > busy myself with Thee."

Look still higher, understand the allusion made in the Verse *He has forgotten them* (IX:67), and you will grasp what happens even to the Beloved overcome by Love. He who understands will understand, but "he who cannot *taste* will never know."

I shall explain this mystery: Love first shows itself in the lover's robe, then clings to the Beloved's skirt. When It finds both sealed with the brand of duality and multiplicity It forces them to turn their eyes away from each other. Then It strips them of the tatters of many-ness and restores to them their true color, the hue of Unity.

> Ah, the rainbow
> > of deception!
> Unity's dying vat will reduce it
> > to a single tint. (Sana'i)

FLASH XXIV

On the fact that the ontological attributes
which belong to the lover are in reality the Attributes
of the Beloved entrusted to the lover, and that
between lover and Beloved
an exchange of Attributes takes place

The lover's search and desire is but a sign of the Beloved's aspiration. Indeed, all his attributes—shame, desire, joy, taste, and laughter—everything he "owns" belongs in truth to the Beloved. The lover but holds it in trust; he cannot even be called a partner, for partnership in attributes would demand two separate essences. But in the

118

lover's contemplative eye there exists in all reality but a single existent Essence.

> A hundred things
> a million or more
> if you look to their reality
> are one.

Thus all attributes pertain to the Beloved alone, leaving no ontological attribute to the lover. How could nonexistence possess the attributes of existence?

Even if the Beloved in His generosity should set foot in the lover's house and brighten it with His Beauty; even if He should bestow on the lover the robe of His own Form, and display Himself to Himself in the lover's guise; even then the lover must not fall into error.

> All is nothing, nothing.
> All, all is HE.

As Ansari put it, "God wished to manifest His handiwork, so He created the world; He wished to manifest Himself, so He created Adam."

FLASH XXV

On the difference between
Knowledge of Certainty, Eye of Certainty, and Truth of Certainty,
and on the levels of Love
in stages

The lover desires to see the Beloved with Certainty's eye, and wanders a bewildered lifetime in this aspiration. Then suddenly with his heart's ear he hears a voice:

> "That magic spring where Khezr
> once drank the water of life
> is in your own home—
> but you have blocked its flow!"

DIVINE FLASHES

Then the Eye of Certainty opens, and staring inwardly at himself, he finds himself lost, vanished. But ... he finds the Friend; and when he looks still deeper, realizes the Friend is himself. He exclaims,

> "Beloved, I sought you
> here and there,
> asked for news of you
> from all I met;
> then saw you through myself
> and found we were identical.
> Now I blush to think I ever
> searched for signs of you."

Everyone with eyes sees just such a vision—but remains ignorant of what he perceives. Every ant which leaves its nest and goes to the desert will see the sun—but not know what it sees. What irony! Everyone perceives Divine Beauty with Certainty's Eye, for in reality nothing exists but Transcendent Unity; they look, they see, but do not comprehend. They take no pleasure in the view, for to enjoy it one must know through the Truth of Certainty what he is seeing, through Whom, and why. *But that my heart may be at peace* (II:262) may allude to such Certainty. Heart's peace and stillness of soul may be realized only through the Truth of Certainty.

"What is Certainty?" they asked Sahl at-Tustari. "God," he replied.

You too, my reader, *Worship thy Lord, until Certainty comes to thee* (XV:99).

> If you lose yourself
> on this path
> you will know in certainty:
> He is you, you are He.

DIVINE FLASHES

FLASH XXVI

*On how the lover focuses attention
upon the Beloved, and on each one's need for the other
in respect of lover-ness and Beloved-ness*

Wishing to focus attention on the Beloved, the lover has no choice but to do so with all his organs and powers of vision; for the Beloved possesses a form on every level of Being, and each of these forms has a Face. In all things he must focus on Divine Self-Manifestation, for not only the Inward but the Outward as well is He: *He is the Outward and the Inward* (LVII:3). The lover must see nothing without seeing God before it—or after it—or within it—or with it.

At this stage, the Retreat, the cell of seclusion is closed to the lover, for he has found the Beloved to be identical with all things. He cannot now choose one station over another nor seclude himself from anything. Why not? The goal of seclusion is to sit in the Retreat of one's own nonexistence, cut off from all one's own names and attributes, hidden from all creatures. But now the lover's being-a-seer has become worthy of the Beloved's being-seen; the lover has realized that the level of being-the-Beloved depends in a sense on his own being-a-lover. How shall he now seek seclusion? "Lordship is impossible without servitude."

So the lover must now rethink his situation: If he is unworthy of the glance of the Beloved, then the Beloved's glance will be empty. For "Truly, Lordship has a secret which would be brought to nothing were it revealed."[29] The exquisite grace of the Beloved may be perfect, and as such in need of nothing—but

> the salesworthiness of your beauty
>> exists because I am your customer—
> isn't it so? What good is an idol
> with no heathen to worship it?

The Divine-as-Beloved needs the lover's gaze.

They asked Sahl at-Tustari, "What does God want of the creatures?" He answered, "Just what they're doing."

121

DIVINE FLASHES

So you see, freedom here is impossible for either side, for when relationship appears, freedom must vanish.

> Freedom and love
> will never mesh—
> so I've become a slave
> and renounced my desire.

Absolute freedom, obviously, is found only at the level of Absolute independence. At the level of the Divine-as-Beloved, however, the lover's helpless need demands the seductive glance of the Beloved, and vice versa. Balance! There must be balance. What does the Beloved mean to say by winking with such seductive charm at the self-abased poverty and dejection of the lover?

> "I exist in a state
> of perfect joy—
> but this state is only fulfilled
> through you."

> "Do not slay me
> for my need is useful.
> Without me, after all, who will remain
> for You to seduce?"

Do you understand their conversation? The tongue of the situation declares,

> "The sultan's honored hand
> takes up the mallet—
> but with no ball on the field
> it doesn't do him much good!"

> No wait . . . I said it wrong.
> Here both lover and Beloved are HE
> even though His Love has reduced us
> to a pretty myth.
> Who are we,
> what can we do?

DIVINE FLASHES

How could we act as mirror for His Face,
   or comb His locks?

FLASH XXVII

*On the beginning
of the lover's direct vision and how the viewer
becomes the viewed*

The lover seeks the Vision in order that he might pass away from existence; he knocks on the door of nonexistence, for there he was once at peace. There he was both seer and seen,

> both viewer and viewed—
>   because nothing in himself.

Coming to be, he became the veil of his own sight and was deprived of Vision. For his sight was the Beloved Himself—"I was his hearing and sight" (HQ)—but his existence is merely a screen to hide this sight.

> Know yourself: a cloud
>   drifting before your sun.
> Cut yourself off from your senses
>   and behold your sun of intimacy.

If this screen—which is you—is struck from before your eyes, the Beloved will find the Beloved, and you will be entirely lost. Then you will hear with the ear of your heart:

> "That mystery, so long concealed
>   is at last opened,
> the darkness of your night at last
>   bathed in dawn.
> You yourself are the veil of the mystery
>   of the Unseen Heart:
> if it were not for you
>   it would never have been sealed."

DIVINE FLASHES

Then you will say:

> "By day I praised You
>   but never knew it;
> by night slept with You
>   without realizing;
> fancying myself
>   to be myself;
> but no, I was You
>   and never knew it."

The lover's prayer: O God, give me light. Bring me to the Station of Vision, that I may know myself as You, and say, "Who sees me, sees God" (H); and that You may reply *Who obeys the Messenger, obeys God* (IV:80). For while I am still myself I shall not see You, and must say, "He is a Light, how shall I see Him?" (H).

> When will He reveal
>   His Face to the world?
> Into what mirror
>   will He fit?

They measured not God with His true measure (VI:91).

FLASH XXVIII

On the transmutation of the lover's attributes,
Subsistence after Annihilation, and the arrival of the lover
at the Station of Articulation after Gathering
and the abode of leading
toward perfection and guiding
toward spirituality

When the Beloved would exalt the lover, He first strips from him the garments collected from all worlds, and clothes him in the robe of His own Attributes. Then the Beloved calls him by all His own Names, and seats him in His own place. Now He may either keep the lover here in this Station of stations,[30] or send him back to the world

to perfect the still-imperfect ones. If He sends him back, He will
clothe him not in the world's colors, which He has stripped away, but
in His own Divine hues.

> Before this there was one heart
> but a thousand thoughts.
> Now all is reduced to
> *There is no god but God.*

When the lover studies his new clothes he finds himself arrayed
in different colors, and will wonder

> "What is this beautiful tint,
> this garment so unique?"

He finds himself perfumed with a new scent, and will marvel:

> "I sense from you an attar
> I cannot recognize.
> Is some sweet girl passing by
> her sleeves drenched in perfume?"

Gazing within himself he will find himself completely Divine, and
will repeat,

> "I am the one I love,
> He Whom I love is I,
> two spirits residing
> in a single body." (al-Hallaj)

Wherever he looks he sees the Friend's Face, and will sing,

> "Everyplace I cast my glance
> I see You.
> Glory be to God!
> Have You become my very eyes?
>
> Are these cups
> sparkling with wine
> or suns casting their glow
> on banks of cloud?"

DIVINE FLASHES

Now he knows the meaning of *Everything is perishing but its face*
(XXVIII:88), and he will know why the pronoun "its" here must refer to "everything"; because everything perishes in its form but
subsists in its meaning, its "face." He will grasp that in one respect
this "face" is the Self-Manifestation of God; for *The face of thy Lord
remains* (LV:27). Dear reader, when you yourself have realized that
the meaning and reality of things is identical with this Divine Countenance, you will pray, "Show us things as they are" (H), and by this
come to see with inward vision that

> in everything there is a sign
> a clue to "He is One."

*Say "Whose is the earth and whoso is in it, if you have knowledge?" They
will say "God's"* (XXIII:86). Verily we belong to Him and subsist
through Him.

If my words seem to smell of drunkenness, pardon me, for they
flow of themselves.

> I drain a cup
> in every subtle meaning
> and by every voice in the universe
> I am filled with delight.

What can I do?

> Every moment my heart
> is tugging me to the tavern;
> how can I remain here
> with these pious hermits?

I have tumbled into a sea whose shores are uncharted. Indeed,

> I am a match
> for the Seven Seas
> though in myself weak
> as a speck of foam.

126

DIVINE FLASHES

And if I seem to repeat myself, forgive me, for whichever way I swim, hoping to cast myself out of this boundless ocean, I cannot find the shore. Sometimes I glimpse it, but the waves steal me away again and hurl me to the abyss.

> Praise be to God
> I live in the sea like a frog:
> If I open my mouth I get
> a mouthful of water;
> If I remain silent
> I die of grief! (Shibli)

I blame myself, for

> There where the waves
> of the endless sea are crashing
> how should the Ocean hobnob
> with a little dewdrop?

But Spiritual Resolve admonishes me: "Hopelessness is by no means obligatory."

> O frog in the unbounded waters,
> struggle on, keep swimming.
> Who knows? Perhaps ... (Sana'i)

The heart swims through the sea of hope, and to the soul which has drawn near its shores it will say,

> "When shall we ,
> divorce ourselves?
> You and I gone
> and only God remain?"

NOTES

1. *Hawd kawthar*, the name of a spring in Paradise. The prophet Khezr is said to have gained everlasting physical life by drinking at the Fountain of Life.

127

DIVINE FLASHES

2. Chapter and verse of Koranic quotations will be indicated thus.

3. All headings are taken from Jami's commentary.

4. "H" indicates a *hadith* or saying of the Prophet, and "HQ" stands for *hadith qudsi:* a prophetic saying that narrates the direct words of God.

5. "His command, when He desires a thing, is to say to it 'Be,' and it is" (xxxvi:81).

6. "God was and nothing was with Him," said the Prophet, and Junayd added, "and He is now as He was!"

7. One of the Prophet's names, signifying "the Chosen One."

8. Sultan Mahmud of Ghazna and his beloved slaveboy Iyaz are stock characters in Persian poetry.

9. I.e., the lover appears wearing the Beloved's cloak, he takes on His Attributes.

10. Continuation of the *hadith* quoted a few lines earlier.

11. Literally "the man of Your love"; cf. "the man of the battlefield", i.e., he who is equal to the challenge.

12. The magic cup of King Jamshid in which he could see anything and everything in the world.

13. Jami explains: "Jesus River is a stream near Baghdad which supplies many farms with irrigation. When abundant rain causes the Tigris to overflow and inundate these farms, they mention this proverb."

14. The first two lines here refer to the second four lines of the poem above, while the second two lines refer to the first four.

15. Jami: The Prophet's *real* "community" are those who have attained the station of Annihilation.

16. *Qut al-qulub* by Abu Talib al-Makki.

17. God's "Acts" are the creatures, which become manifest within the world as a result of the ontological possibilities represented by the Attributes.

18. The word in the Koranic verse translated as "forgiveness" (*maghfarah*) according to its root meaning signifies "covering."

19. That is, those Names that are the basis for the very possibility of created existence. See Commentary, note 30.

20. The first "year" is the Most Holy Effusion. This is what the man meant when he asked, "Who was it then prepared you first?" The second "year" is the Holy Effusion, by which man "comes forward in servitude" in the external world.

21. Since the "creation of nonexistence" is not the same sort of creation as the "creation of existence," 'Iraqi explains the difference in the next paragraph to prevent any confusion.

22. There is a play on words between "inadequacy" (*qusur*) and "palaces" (*qusur*).

23. *Waqt*, "time" or "spiritual state of the moment." *As-sufi ibn al-waqt:* "The Sufi is the child of the moment."

24. This line, which does not occur in all manuscripts, is according to Jami a *hadith qudsi*. The idea is that the master depends on the slaves, for without slaves how could he be a "master"?

25. Jami interprets: He remains an immutable archetypal-entity in God's Knowledge with no existence in the world.

26. "Make use of the Greatest Blackness" is a *hadith*, although some people have interpreted it to mean "Avoid the Greatest Blackness."

27. I.e., "I took refuge in Him but it was He taking refuge in Himself."

28. I.e., "Though I praise Thee, it is really Thou praising Thyself." This sentence is a continuation of the *hadith* cited a few lines earlier.

29. The saying, often quoted by Ibn al-'Arabi, is by Sahl at-Tustari. It means that a revealed secret is no longer a secret. The secret of Lordship is that there must be servants. No servants, no Lord.

30. I.e., annihilation in the Vision of the All-comprehensive Essence (Jami).

Commentary on the Divine Flashes

PROLOGUE

'Iraqi begins his treatise in the manner of any other traditional Moslem author: by praising God and asking Him to bless the Prophet. But like most authors, he alludes to the principles and gist of what he wants to discuss in the midst of the conventional opening. In short, he describes the Perfect Man, or rather the prototype of all Perfect Men, the Prophet of Islam, as the object of God's Love and the locus in which the Name-derived Perfection is actualized.

After the praise and blessing, 'Iraqi turns to the third conventional element in the prologue of any work: the statement of purpose. Here he describes Love in terms that make explicit its identification with God Himself. He states that only Love exists, and he asserts that all things are the loci-of-manifestation for the Attributes and perfections of Love. So all creatures, all lovers and beloveds, are nothing but the Self-Manifestations of Love.

INTRODUCTION

Here 'Iraqi identifies Love (whether we use the term *hubb* or *'ishq*), even more explicitly with the Nonentified Essence, Being as such. He explains that the whole of the *Lama'at* is nothing but a discussion of Love's entifications.

In referring to the journey of Love through the stages of "repose" and "lodging," 'Iraqi is alluding to the teachings of Qunawi, who in turn derives his terminology from the verse, "It is He who produced you from one living soul, and then (placed you in) a lodging place, and then a repository" (VI:98). That "one soul" is the First Entification, that is, the reality of Adam or the Perfect Man. But for the reality (= archetypal-entity) to enter into the world, it must pass

COMMENTARY

through the Divine Presences. In other words, it must "descend" from the Knowledge of God (the First Presence), to the Presence of the Spirits, then to the Presence of Image-Exemplars, and finally to the Presence of the Corporeal World. Through this descent man's reality actualizes all the different kinds of outward manifestation. But they are dispersed and multiple. In order to attain their unification and to live in oneness, man must return to the Divine through the Way. He must actualize the Fifth Presence by becoming the Perfect Man. So this is the "Bow of Ascent," which complements the "Bow of Descent" (cf. Flash XIV). In Qunawi's teaching, the "lodging places" refer to the various stages of the descent. The "repository" refers to the womb, where man finally attains a perfect outward form, made in God's image. The womb is the final stage in the "descent" of the First Entification and at the same time the first stage in its ascent (see the commentary on Flash XXVIII).

FLASH I

Since "Love" in 'Iraqi's terminology refers to Being as such, it is the source of all things. The lover or creature, who is the "possible-existent" (*mumkin*), derives from Being, just as the Beloved or God (the "Necessary-Being": *wajib*) is also nothing but Being, although delimited in a certain sense—for God is Necessary and not possible or contingent. But Being is beyond delimitation by either Necessity or possibility, so It embraces both God and the world. Thus Love is the source of both lover and Beloved. Moreover, the Arabic words "lover" (*'ashiq*) and "beloved" (*ma'shuq*) both derive from the root "love" (*'ishq*).

In this Flash 'Iraqi employs the terms "outward" and "inward" in a manner that may seem puzzling. Usually, when the "Outward of Being" is mentioned, the total unfolding and manifestation of Being in keeping with Its inherent perfections—that is, the totality of creation—is meant. This is contrasted with Being's "Inward," which refers to Being in Its station of Nonentification. But sometimes the "Inward" of Being refers to the infinite possibilities of manifestation latent within Being, or in other words, to the archetypal-entities at the level of their "nonexistence" in God's Knowledge. From this point of view, the things always remain nonexistent, and what becomes outwardly manifest is only Being, or Being as colored by the effects of the entities. For in reality, "The entities have never smelt

131

COMMENTARY

the fragrance of existence" (Ibn al-'Arabi). So in this respect the "Outward of Being" refers to Being as such, since nothing else exists. The entities always remain "inward" and nonexistent.[1]

At the end of the first paragraph of the Flash, 'Iraqi refers to this less common usage of the terms "inward" and "outward." He says that Love manifested Itself to the nonexistent entities, that is, the lovers or possible existents. Thus the entities came into existence and their fame was established. Before coming into existence they were known only to God, whereas after existence they became known to others as well. Likewise, when Love through Its theophanies showed Itself within the outward world, It became known as the Beloved. Having displayed the Outward (Being) to the Inward (the existent-entities), Love caused the Outward/Beloved to become the object of the Inward/lovers' desire.

In the poem that follows the first paragraph, 'Iraqi reverts to the first and more common usage of the terms "Outward" and "Inward," making the lover outward and the Beloved inward. Obviously 'Iraqi wants both meanings to be contemplated. Moreover, the juxtaposition of the two meanings emphasizes the essential ambiguity of the situation, where in fact all three—loved, Beloved, and Love—are one.

Although we have already discussed 'Iraqi's description of Love as the source of all things, it may be useful to reconsider it in the light of his remarks here.

In the First Entification, Nondelimited Being, or the Unseen Essence of God, "manifested Itself to Itself in theophany." As a result, Knowledge of God's Essence and all Its concomitants became actualized. Once these concomitants—or "Names and Attributes"—are entified, they become the source for all the creatures. Considered as the principles of each and every thing, they are usually referred to as the "immutable archetypal-entities." They are also called "possible-existents" (*mumkinat*), since God may bestow being upon them if He so desires. But as long as they do not manifest their effects within the world but remain known only to God, they are said to be "nonexistent."

'Iraqi alludes to the fact that when the Essence—Love—manifested Itself to Itself, a certain kind of "relational many-ness" could be observed in the midst of Oneness. In other words, Oneness embraces all possibilities at the level of Inclusive-Unity. This many-ness is called "relational" because the Names and Attributes are also referred to as "relations." Each of them gives news of a certain interrelationship that may exist among various realities. Thus, when God gazed on Himself through the Attributes or relations of Vision and Knowledge, He became Viewer and Viewed, Knower and Known. At the same time, His essence remained Unseen and Unknown. So He became both Outwardly Manifest and Inwardly Nonmanifest. Hence the basic duality from which many-ness derives—God as the "Outward" and God as the "Inward"—was established. Through the Name "Outward" the world became entified and acted as a receptacle for being. The Name "Inward" reminds us that He remains Nonentified and Transcendent in Himself.

In addition, God is Love. So the very creation of the universe derives from this Attribute, since He "loved" to be known. The relation of Love implies a Lover and a Beloved, and at the level of the First Entification where Love is first actualized, Lover and Beloved can be none but He, since this is also the level of Oneness. What He loved was His own infinite Beauty and the never-ending possibilities of outward manifestation and deployment latent within it, or, in other words, the Perfection of Distinct-Manifestation and Distinct-Vision. He wanted His own infinite beauties and perfections to be spread out in an unlimited extension and deployment so that what He viewed within Himself at the level of the Name "Inward" (i.e., the Hidden Treasure) might also be viewed "without" Himself at the level of the Name "Outward."

But in reality, none has Being but God. The entities are nonexistent. So the viewer in truth is He, just as the viewed is none but He. "God is Beautiful, and He Loves Beauty" (H). He is Being, and He loves Being and all that shares in It. So He loves the world, since it "exists," and its existence is none other than His Being, since Being is One.

Since Being is Love, Love pervades all the Presences and all the existent-entities. Moreover, since God loves Beauty, "loverness" pervades all things as well. And likewise Beauty—"Belovedness"—is also all-pervasive. So all things reflect God's Love, just as they reflect Loverness and Belovedness, since these three Attributes brought them into existence and moreover pertain to existence itself.

In short, there is but One Reality: Love or Being. It manifests Itself in two forms, the lover and the Beloved, man and God. The two reflect each other, observe each other, and love each other, thus mak-

COMMENTARY

ing God's Names and Attributes—the Hidden Treasure—manifest. As a result all the latent perfections of Being become outwardly known.

FLASH II

The entities or things have no existence of their own. Being belongs only to God. So the immutable archetypal-entities are called "nonexistent objects of Knowledge." But these nonexistent entities are precisely the possibilities of Self-Manifestation latent within Being, possibilities that become clearly differentiated from one another at the level of Inclusive-Unity. They are the Hidden Treasure, and since God "loved to be known," He bestowed being on them and they entered into the world.

So God the Beloved displayed Himself through theophany and outward-manifestation to the nonexistent archetypal-entities. Just as the things became entified within His Knowledge in the first place through the "Unseen Theophany" or the "Most Holy Effusion," so now they come into existence through the "Visible Theophany" or "Holy Effusion," also known as the "Second Entification." Each of the archetypal-entities manifests itself in the world as a different existent-entity. In their state of nonexistence in Knowledge, the entities were one; all opposites coincided. But when they enter existence, each possesses a different locus-of-manifestation, so the world is filled with opposition, strife and tumult.

After explaining how Love manifested Itself to the lover, as a result of which the world came into being through the Visible Theophany, 'Iraqi then alludes to the Most Holy Effusion with his words "the splendor of Beauty," that is, the theophany through which the lover had received the preparedness to act as a receptacle for Being in the first place. It is not as if the lover existed separately from the Beloved before he entered into the world. On the contrary, the lover was necessarily entified within Knowledge beforehand in order for him to be able to "see" the Beloved when He manifested Himself to him in the second place. Only through His Light can one see Him. Only through the preparedness He had already bestowed on the entity can the entity act as a receptacle for His Being.

Then 'Iraqi refers to the identity of Light and Being. When God sprinkled being on the nonexistent entities, the earth—that is, the creatures, the things—came into existence. Having entered into out-ward-manifestation, the lover immediately sets out in quest of his Be-loved. Finding Him, he realizes that nothing has changed, all is as it was, the lover is still nonexistent and only Being *is*.

The careful reader might be puzzled by 'Iraqi's ascription of per-ception to the "nonexistent" entity in the paragraph beginning, "When the lover grasped. . . ." This is an allusion to the fact that in this state, the entity participates in God's Being within His Knowl-edge and therefore possesses in a certain respect the ontological per-fections, such as life and knowledge. Jami points out that in the *Futuhat* (vol. 3, p. 257), Ibn al-'Arabi also speaks of the archetypal-enti-ties as possessing qualities such as sight and hearing.

FLASH III

The Perfection of Distinct-Manifestation is the Outward-Mani-festation of the Being of God through the entities, which are the loci for His Theophany—first, for the Unseen Theophany of Knowledge, and second, for the Visible Theophany in the world. When the exis-tent-entities become deployed through this second Theophany, the Perfection of Distinct-Manifestation is achieved. But God "loved to be *known*." It is not enough for the infinite possibilities of Self-Mani-festation to be deployed, they must also be perceived and contemplat-ed. This is the "Perfection of Distinct-Vision," which is realized only through the Perfect Man, the mirror for the totality of the Names and Attributes.

But for man to attain this Perfection, within which he contem-plates Being and all Its perfections, and because of which Being con-templates Itself within him, he must first be delivered from his illusory selfhood. As long as he is dominated by his ego and his own individuality, he will never reach his true station. He must enter the Path and annihilate all his own illusory attributes, so that they may be replaced by his true attributes, which are nothing but the Attri-butes of Being as such.

In Itself Being is Sheer Oneness. But since the entity has achieved a certain kind of independent existence through the Visible Theophany—even though its being can be none other than the Being of God, since Being is One—duality and multiplicity have appeared within Being. For the existent-entity requires a Source and a Place of

COMMENTARY

Return, a Beginning and an End. In respect of the fact that It is the Source, Being is "Eternity-without-Beginning," and since It is the Place of Return, It is "Eternity-without-End."

FLASH IV

God's "Jealousy" (*ghayrat*) is a result of the Might of His Unity and the All-Subjugating Power of His Oneness. "God was, and nothing was with Him." Having heard these words of the Prophet, Junayd added, "And He is now as He was." God's Might does not allow any "others" (*ghayr*) to have existence.

As long as an atom of us remains, Thy Might
will not allow Thy Beauty to be displayed.[2]

Being is One, and Being is God's. So no one else *is*. When the gnostic attains the station of the annihilation of his illusory existence in God, he experiences the "Greatest Resurrection" and understands the meaning of the verse, " 'Whose is the Dominion today (at the Resurrection)?' 'God's, the One, the All-Subjugating' " (XL:16).[3]

So any entity that seems to possess an attribute or property in reality possesses nothing at all. For God *is*, and nothing *is* with Him. The attributes of the entities were established by the Unseen Theophany, and their existence was given to them by the Visible Theophany. But the two theophanies are in fact nothing but the One Effusion from the One, for Being is One, and all Its Attributes and Names are nothing but the manifestation of the nature of that Oneness. All attributes, names, properties, relations, aspects, modes, and delineations attributed to the creatures are only the concomitants of His One Being. He Himself plays all parts.

FLASH V

The Nonentified Being of God can assume every possible entification. The perfections of Being are infinite, since all things, all entities, all attributes, all descriptions, all delineations, all delimitations, derive from It, while It is Nondelimited. In addition, the absolute Oneness of God demands the infinite many-ness of His Self-Manifestations. Each locus of theophany is nothing but the One. So each is unique, which is to say that each is different from every other. In each locus at each instant another perfection of Infinite Being is revealed. Both time and space are modes of deployment of God's perfections within the World of the Visible. Just as no two points in space, no two objects, are exactly alike in every respect—otherwise they would be the same entity and would not exist in two different places—so no two points in time are exactly alike. Therefore Ibn al-'Arabi and his followers speak of the "renewal of creation at each instant." This does not mean that there is no relation between an existent-being's states in two consecutive instants. In fact, every existent-entity reflects the unfolding of a single archetypal-entity or reality, whose possibilities of ontological perfection are perceived in this world as constant transformations, since deployment here takes place in a temporal mode. But the entity itself remains one; only its attributes and outward manifestations undergo change. If this were not the case, religion could not speak of heaven and hell in any meaningful sense, for one entity would perform the acts and a second entity would suffer the consequences.

This whole Flash may be said to be a commentary on the well-known Sufi saying, "Theophany never repeats itself" (*la takrar fi-t-tajalli*).

The statement " 'One' is the fountainhead of all numbers" refers to the fact that in Islamic mathematics, "one" is not in itself a numeral, but is free of all delimitation and determination. "One" therefore can become "entified" by the forms of the infinite series of numerals (i.e., as new "perplexities"). If "one" were *in itself* delimited and determined, it could not assume these myriad forms. It would exist alone and by itself, and the numbers could not come into being. By analogy, Love in Its Absolute Nonentification can take on any face. Thus is the world of multiplicity created.

As for 'Iraqi's statement that only the "Possessor of the Heart" receives insight into the Divine transmutations, here he is following Ibn al-'Arabi's explanation of the nature of the Heart (*al-qalb*) in the twelfth chapter of the *Fusus*. The basic meaning of the word, he says, is indicated by the term "transmutation" (*taqallub*), which derives from the same Arabic root. Within the Heart God reveals Himself to man in never-repeating theophanies.

FLASH VI

Here 'Iraqi discusses one of the highest spiritual stations in Sufism, known technically as the "All-Comprehensiveness of All-Comprehensiveness" (*jam' al-jam'*) or "Two Bows' Length" (*qab qawsayn:*

COMMENTARY

see Commentary on Flash XIV). It is the station of Perfection attained by the greatest Perfect Men, that is, many of the prophets and some of the great saints. Beyond it is only the Station of the "Unity of All-Comprehensiveness" (*ahadiyyat al-jam'*), also called "Or Nearer" (*aw adna*), a station that belongs exclusively to the Prophet of Islam and certain of his inheritors. Farghani's lengthy commentary on Ibn al-Farid's "Poem of the Way" describes these stations extensively.

As 'Iraqi points out, this station—which is the end of the Path for most of the Perfect Men—possesses two characteristics: On the one hand the lover or the Perfect Man sees the Beloved as his own mirror, so he witnesses all his own perfections and properties reflected in God; and on the other hand the lover sees himself as the mirror of the Beloved, so he contemplates all the Attributes of God in himself.

This station of perfection comprehends and contains two lower stations of limited perfection, each of which must be passed through and each of which corresponds to one of its two characteristics.[4] The first of the lower stations is called the "Proximity of Supererogatory-Works" (*qurb an-nawafil*). Since man himself is apparently the agent who chooses which works to perform in order to attain this proximity, it results in a station where the wayfarer's reality still subsists, although it is completely dominated by God's Oneness and becomes qualified by His Attributes and properties. Here God manifests Himself in accordance with His Name "Inward", so that He remains hidden within the lover. The agent and subject of all perception is the lover, while God's presence within him is manifested by the fact that He becomes the lover's faculties. This station is referred to by the following *hadith qudsi:* "The servant never ceases gaining proximity to Me through supererogatory works until I love him. Then when I love him, I am his hearing and his sight: he hears through Me, sees through Me and exercises his reason through Me." 'Iraqi refers to this station with his words, "Sometimes the Beloved becomes the lover's sight."

The second of the lower stations is known as the "Proximity of Obligatory-Works" (*qurb al-fara'id*). Since God Himself takes the initiative directly by prescribing the works that must be performed to attain this kind of proximity, it results in the annihilation of the servant's reality, although his properties remain. God manifests Himself in keeping with the Name "Outward," so the lover remains hidden within Him. The subject and agent is God, whereas the lover's hid-

138

den presence is manifested by his becoming God's faculties. The Prophet referred to this station in the *hadith*, "God says with the tongue of his servant. . . ." 'Iraqi alludes to it in the sentence, "Sometimes the lover becomes the Beloved's voice."

Some of the words attributed to the Beloved in the last paragraph are taken from a story related in traditional sources about the prophet David. God says to him, "O David! Tell those who claim for themselves My love that they must not have doubts about Me at their mealtimes. Hast thou ever seen a lover niggardly toward his lover? Is not the desire of the pious drawn out endlessly, their desire to meet Me? But verily I desire them more than they desire Me!"[5]

FLASH VII

All things are the Self-Manifestation of Being, so whatever is loved is identical with God, the Beloved. It is impossible for anyone to love anything else, since nothing else *is*. The object of love—beauty, or goodness—is nothing but God's Attribute. Just as "There is no reality but God," so also "There is no beauty but God," "There is no goodness but God."

And since nothing else exists, the subject or lover is also God. The whole drama of lover and Beloved is played by One Reality, in order that He may display the Hidden Treasure and then know it through various kinds of knowledge that are realizable only after the full deployment of Outward-Manifestation and the intervention of intermediate causes and the ontological levels and Presences.

Moreover, when God views Himself in the things, He views *Himself,* not part of Himself or an Attribute of Himself. Each thing possesses all of His Attributes, for "Being descends with all Its soldiers." Each thing that *is,* by that very fact is Being. So it possesses all Being's perfections. However, each thing does not display all Being's perfections outwardly, since only the Perfect Man has the preparedness to act as a receptacle and mirror for Being as such. All other things keep most of Being's perfections and properties hidden within themselves.

Being is none other than Sheer Light, and physical light displays many of its characteristics. The objects that become illuminated by light normally absorb most of its possibilities of outward manifestation and reflect only one of them, which is displayed as a particular

COMMENTARY

color. So also most of Being's perfections remain inward and non-manifest in any given thing. Only man has the capacity to attain a station where he can act as a reflector for Sheer Light. But in any case, through the Perfection of Distinct-Vision, God contemplates all His Attributes in every atom.

Jami explains the meaning of 'Iraqi's statement that the cause of love springing from man's every essence (*mahabbat-i dhati*) is unknown—a point often mentioned by Qunawi and Farghani—as follows: "The object of such a love is none but the Essence of God. Clearly, every essence is a shadow and branch of God's Essence. So the essence's love is reducible to the Love deriving from God's Essence. For 'Iraqi, this point is self-evident, or else he would have had to prove it." Jami is saying that love springing from the lover's essence has no cause because it is identical with God's own Love, and God's own Love is nothing but His very Self. And the "Cause of causes" has no cause Himself.

As for Layla and Majnun, they are the archetypal lovers of Persian poetry and died without consummating their love. The *hadith* indicates that they died martyrs and hence were assured of Paradise. Jami interprets its meaning as follows: "Whoever has been so infatuated (*mahabbat*) with physical beauty as to be drawn into love (*'ishq*), but has not taken the pleasures of carnal desire, nor spoken to anyone with the aim of finding a solution (to his problem), so that the grief remains fixed in his heart and he dies of it, has gained the felicity of martyrdom."

The point 'Iraqi wants to make concerning the Prophet's saying "The believer is the mirror of the believer" and the fact that "Believer" is one of God's Names (although it is usually translated as "All-Faithful" or "Keeper of Faith") is explained by Jami: The fact that God sees nothing but himself in the mirror of the servant depends on reading the *hadith* so that the first "believer" refers to the servant and the second to God. As for the fact that the slave sees nothing but himself in the mirror of God's Being, this depends on taking the first "believer" to refer to God and the second to the servant. But if we take both "believers" to refer to God, the *hadith* reveals that viewer, viewed, and mirror are all God.

Finally, Jami explains why lover and Beloved are one: "That-Which-Manifests-Itself and the locus-of-manifestation are different in themselves, and also in terms of the Nondelimitation of the former

140

COMMENTARY

and the delimitation of the latter. But in terms of manifestation they are one, since That-Which-Manifests-Itself within some locus-of-manifestation must also *be* that very locus, for without that locus It could not manifest Itself. The Shaykh (Ibn al-'Arabi) writes in his *Futuhat,* 'So He is identical with all things in manifestation, though not the same as all things in their essences. On the contrary, He is He, and the things are the things.' "

FLASH VIII

In this Flash 'Iraqi alludes to the different stages of "unveiling" as well as to the stations of "annihilation" (*fana'*) and "subsistence" (*baqa'*)[6] and the affinity between Beauty and form on the one hand and Majesty and meaning on the other.

Unveiling, or direct vision of the "mysteries" and realities of things, is usually divided into two main kinds: "formal" and "supraformal," or "form-related" (*suri*) and "meaning-related" (*ma'nawi*). The "form" of something is its outward, visible manifestation, whereas its "meaning" is its inward, unseen dimension, or its mystery. Usually, in fact, the meaning of something is its archetypal-entity.

Here it may be useful to point out that all three of the above pairs of terms, and others like them, are correlative. This means that when we speak of the dualities "outward-inward," "visible-unseen," "form-meaning," dualities that are more or less synonymous, we must always study the context to determine exactly which level is meant. In general, the unseen, inward, and supraformal as such is the First Presence, the World of God's Knowledge; whereas the relatively unseen, inward, and supraformal is the World of the Spirits. Then the absolutely visible, outward, and formal is the World of Corporeal-Bodies, while the relatively visible, outward, and formal is the World of Image-Exemplars. But at the same time, the World of the Spirits is visible, outward, and formal in relation to the Presence of Knowledge, and the World of Image-Exemplars is unseen, inward and supraformal in relation to the World of Sensory-Perception.

Here by "supraformal" 'Iraqi seems to mean the World of the Spirits. Thus we can conclude that by the third kind of theophany, he may be referring to the unveiling of the World of Divine Knowledge, which would then correspond to the station of "Two Bows' Length." But by "supraformal" he may be alluding to the unveiling of the

COMMENTARY

World of Meanings or Knowledge, not the World of Spirits. In this case the third station will refer to the theophany of the Essence Itself, or the station of "Or Nearer." In his commentary on this passage, Jami seems puzzled as to the exact distinction between the second and third kind of unveiling that 'Iraqi mentions. He can only suggest that the third station is more perfect than the second.

FLASH IX

After referring once again to the fact that the Perfect Man and God are mirror images of one another, 'Iraqi turns to an explanation of some of the kinds of theophany and unveiling the gnostic may experience in his Wayfaring.

In the first paragraph he alludes to the identity of the Names and Attributes with the Essence. For each Name in its reality can be nothing but Being, the only Reality there is. Thus the "Living" is none other than the Divine Self, since "None has life but God"; and so on with all the Names. But from a certain point of view—to which 'Iraqi does not refer here—the Names are indeed different, for each requires a different locus-of-manifestation in the world. In its act, the "Giver of Life" (al-muhyi) is different from the "Giver of Death" (al-mumit), although in essence they are the same.

As Jami points out, much of the discussion of this Flash is a translation and summary of a section from Ibn al-'Arabi's *Futuhat*. In order to illustrate one way in which 'Iraqi makes use of the teachings of Ibn al-'Arabi and his followers, we provide below a literal and complete translation of this passage.

After quoting from Ibn al-'Arabi, 'Iraqi states in the last paragraph of the Flash that in any case, supraformal unveiling is higher than formal unveiling, so the lover should not be satisfied with anything less. He should strive to attain the station of the great Perfect Men and to contemplate God without any intermediaries.

In the passage 'Iraqi quotes from the *Futuhat*, Ibn al-'Arabi is discussing the ontological perfection that is manifested by the Divine Name "Peace" (as-salam). He wants to point out that whoever experiences the theophany of this Name will partake of its properties. At the same time, he connects this theophany to the Proximity of Supererogatory Works, which was referred to in the commentary on Flash VII. He states that when someone truly experiences the theophany of

142

COMMENTARY

"Peace," he will be released from individual limitations and participate in this Proximity, where God becomes his faculties and sense organs.

Ibn al-'Arabi writes: "God says, 'Theirs is the Abode of Peace'
(VI:127). It is an abode within which no weariness strikes them, so
within it they are at peace. You should know that the gnostic's peace
is his being absolutely beyond making any claim to lordship, except
that its inspirational breaths become manifest to him in the station of
direct-vision where God becomes all his faculties, so this is a kind of
claim. Hence in this the servant is 'at peace' from his own self. Because of this kind of peace, 'Peace' is a Divine Name. When the Companions wanted to say, 'Peace be upon God,' the Prophet said, 'Do
not say, "Peace be upon God," for God, He is Peace.'

"So when the servant—who is the 'Servant of Peace'—becomes
present with God in the Presence of this Name such that God is his
mirror, let him contemplate the form he sees therein. If he should see
within the mirror an inward form and a view made up of the shape of
his own outward, he will know that he sees himself and that he has
not actualized the degree of that person for whom God has become all
the faculties. But if he should see a form which is not made up of a
corporeal shape, while at the same time he should understand that
there is something not identical with himself, then that form is a form
of God. The servant at this time may have realized the station where
God is his faculties.

"If in this direct-vision the servant is identical with the mirror
and God has manifested Himself within him through theophany,
then let him contemplate what has manifested itself within him in respect of his being a mirror. If a theophany is manifested within him
delimited by his shape, then the domination belongs to the mirror
(i.e., himself), not to God. For the Viewer (whose form is reflected in
the mirror) may become delimited by the reality of the mirror's
shape: its length, width, roundness, curvature, largeness and small-
ness. So the mirror will reflect the Viewer within itself, but it will
dominate over His form. So the servant will know from the delimitation in accordance with the shape of the mirror that what he saw
could have9undergone transformations within the shape of his form
in the different kinds (of transformations) that his reality allows in
that state. But if he should see the theophany outside of the shape of
his own essence, he should know that it is God, He who 'eccompasses

all things' (IV:126). In whatever form God becomes manifest, the servant will be at peace from the effect of other forms within him, because the 'Presence of Peace' bestows that."[7]

FLASH X

In his famous dictum Ibn al-'Arabi declares, "The entities have never smelt—and will never smell—the fragrance of existence." The entities can never exist in themselves, since they are only the infinite modes of the One Being's Perfections. Being as such is nondelimited, nonentified, nondefined. Each of the entities, however, represents only one mode of Being's perfection. So in a certain sense each is a definition, delimitation, and constriction of Being. These limitations, which Being takes on Itself by Its very nature, cause each of Its perfections to be displayed outwardly in a separate locus-of-theophany. In much the same way, colored objects allow us to contemplate the perfections or possibilities of manifestation—the colors—hidden within pure light. For each object can act only as a receptacle for some of light's possibilities. Each delimits and defines light and makes its intrinsic perfections known to us. The colors themselves belong to the light, since it is only that same light which becomes outwardly manifest, albeit delimited and defined. It is not the *objects* we see— they remain hidden—but only the perfections of light that are reflected from them. In the same way, the entities own nothing of their own. They are only limitations imposed on Being by virtue of the Name-derived Perfection inherent within Being's Essence.

In short, we must always remember that the things, the entities, the "existents," have no existence of their own. They always remain nonexistent and therefore nonmanifest and inward. What becomes outwardly manifest is Being delimited by the effects of the entities.[8]

After discussing the theoretical dimension of the entities' nonexistence, 'Iraqi turns his main attention to the practical application of this teaching to the Sufi Path. Multiplicity, separation, diversity, differentiation, conflict, strife—all pertain to the entities. But the Traveler's goal is to escape nonexistence and be drowned in Sheer Being, in which all opposites coincide and disappear. "Things" are precisely entities, so in fact they have no being of their own. At the level of Oneness and Being, the properties of thingness and entification are transcended.

Through Wayfaring the Sufi must return to his own Source,

COMMENTARY

which is "nonexistence." But in no way does nonexistence—the state of being an object of God's Knowledge—imply deprivation; quite the opposite. For the principle of "nonexistence" is Being Itself. The nonexistent things are nothing but modes of perfection of God's Being. Annihilation of the entity means subsistence as a mode of perfection within God. While retaining all the ontological perfections manifested by his own archetypal-entity, the Traveler is reunited with the source of those perfections, that is, Being Itself. Ultimately he becomes the Perfect Man, the immediate and conscious mirror of all the perfections of Being. In this station, he has no attributes, since he has no being, no essence.[9] Only God has Being, and only His Essence has Attributes. There are no things or entities, Bayazids or 'Iraqis, who might have some sort of reality independent of God's Reality. There is no essence that might say, "I—Bayazid—am." On the contrary, the Attribute of God known as "Bayazid" can only say, "There is nothing in my robe but God."

As for the meaning of the enigmatic verse at the beginning, Jami explains it as follows: The verse is spoken by the lover. "My mother" is the archetypal-entity; "her father" is the Beloved, Nondelimited Being. "The lover's mother gave birth to her own father because his immutable archetypal-entity became entified through Nondelimited Being's Unseen Theophany of Knowledge. So in respect of this theophany, Nondelimited Being is the parent of the immutable entity. As for the birth of Nondelimited Being from the immutable entity, this occurs because after becoming manifested, It is colored by the properties of the immutable entity. So in respect of delimitation and being colored by its properties, Nondelimited Being is born from the immutable entity."

FLASH XI

Here 'Iraqi wants to make clear that Union with the Beloved does not imply "unificationism" (*ittihad*) or "incarnationism" (*hulul*), two heresies that have been condemned throughout Islamic history by theologians, philosophers, and Sufis. The first of these two terms means that two things come together and become one thing, and the second that one thing enters into another. In order to show the falsity of these ideas, 'Iraqi first points out that what really occurs is the Self-Manifestation of God through theophany, a process that can be compared to an image reflected within a mirror. No one ever says that the

145

COMMENTARY

image is "incarnated within" or "united with" the mirror. In fact, the example is somewhat defective, since it implies that two things—the image and the mirror—exist separately. But in the case of theophany only God has Being, and only Being is perceived, although It is colored by the effects of the entities. So the mirror-entities are nonexistent. Only the image-Being *is*.

So from another point of view, we see that no entity truly exists. The entity itself is only the Self-Manifestation of Being. Hence the true situation contradicts the very definitions of incarnationism and unificationism, both of which imply the existence of two different things.[10]

FLASH XII

The "opening of the door" is a reference to "Opening" (*fath*), one of the technical terms of Ibn al-'Arabi's school, which implies the arrival at a station on the Way where Union dominates over separation and man no longer travels *toward* God. From here on he travels *in* and *through* God.[11] There is no longer any goal outside of himself after which man can strive. The journey is now from one Self-Manifestation of God to another, from the theophany of one Attribute to the theophany of another. Man now turns toward the station of "bewilderment," within which the theophanies of God's perfections never repeat themselves. Through a never-ending succession of Self-Manifestations, man's heart (*qalb*) undergoes perpetual transmutation (*taqallub*) as he participates in the Self-Unfolding of the Hidden Treasure.[12]

As 'Iraqi states in the first poem, when the Heart becomes purified, it has no more any need to travel toward the Beloved, since it now reflects the Beloved within itself. When man attains this station, all created and generated attributes have been erased from him. He arrives at the station of Subsistence (*baqa'*), within which he manifests only God's Attributes, without intermediary. He no longer needs to travel on the path of asceticism and purification, since by his very nature he is a direct and conscious Self-Manifestation of God.

FLASH XIII

The "veil" is one of the Sufis' favorite images. Here 'Iraqi indicates his preference for the interpretation of its meaning given by Ibn

COMMENTARY

al-'Arabi and his followers. God's veils are His very Names and Attributes. In one respect they are luminous, since they are the perfections of Sheer Being—which is Light—radiating forth. They display Its very nature to us. But in another respect they are tenebrous, since the Names and Attributes are also different from God: Each of them (except the Greatest Name) is the manifestation of a single ontological perfection. So when we behold God's Names and Attributes, we see the perfections of Being, not Being Itself. In exactly the same way, each thing manifests Being—for nothing else exists—but at the same time hides It from the creatures, for instead of Nonentification we see entities.[13]

In short: The very intensity of God's Light—His Self-Manifestation—veils His Self. For the Names and Attributes, which appear to us in the guise of the entities, hide the Nonentified Essence.

FLASH XIV

Concerning the Prophet's ascent to God (mi'raj), the Koran states, he "drew near and suspended hung, two bows' length away, or nearer" (LIII:8–9). Much of the discussion of the spiritual ascent in Ibn al-'Arabi's school centers around these two stations of "Two Bows' Length" and "Or Nearer."[14] According to Qunawi, the Two Bows are Oneness and many-ness, or Necessary-Being and possible-existence, or Being and the Divine Knowledge that has as its object the possible things.[15] These correspond to the two great entifications of Nonentified Being: the Unseen and the Visible. Together these two Presences form the Circle of Being, by which all entifications of Sheer Being are comprehended.[16]

'Iraqi states that the differentiation between the two bows or arcs of the Circle can be represented by a line bisecting the Circle. But Being is One, and this bisection derives only from the possibilities of Self-Manifestation inherent within Being's very nature. In no way does it bring about true duality. Necessary-Being and possible-existence are two perfections latent within Being Itself.

When the Wayfarer attains the contemplation of the One Being, the differentiation between the two Presences is effaced. He realizes that Being is One and assumes different aspects and modes in Its Self-Manifestation. This contemplation, when truly realized, is called the station of Two Bows' Length. But a certain duality is still implied, for it is the lover who is contemplating the Beloved and who realizes this

COMMENTARY

vision. So the effect of the line that bisects the Circle still remains to some degree. We still have three things: lover, Beloved, and love or union.

But God's Absolute Oneness is such that it can allow no many-ness to subsist. "God is, and nothing is with Him." So another station still remains, about which 'Iraqi prefers to keep silent. As Jami points out, he is referring to the station of "Or Nearer," the highest degree man can attain. According to Farghani, the station of Two Bows' Length "makes the two bows (of Necessary-Being and possible-existence) into a single connected Circle, but a hidden trace of multiplicity remains between the two. But the inward of this station—the station of 'Or Nearer,' i.e., nearer than the proximity of Two Bows' Length—leaves no trace of differentiation and multiplicity in the Circle."[17]

Having discussed these stations, 'Iraqi next turns to an analysis of the meaning of "Unity" and the reason that Unity can remain even when there is a servant who realizes It. First he mentions Ibn al-'Arabi's distinction between two kinds of Unity. In the *Fusus* he writes, "The Unity of God in respect to the Divine Names, which seek us (i.e., which demand our existence, since they represent the possibilities of God's Self-Manifestation), is the 'Unity of Manyness,' while the Unity of God in respect to His Independence from us and from the Names is the 'Unity of Entity.' Concerning both, the word 'one' (*ahad*) is employed."[18] These two are essentially the same as the two points of view from which the Oneness of the First Entification can be considered, that is, Exclusive-Unity, where all many-ness is effaced by the One Being, and Inclusive-Unity, within which all ontological perfections are contained. Qunawi often refers to these two points of view as "True Oneness," in opposition to which no many-ness can be envisaged, and "numerical oneness," in respect to which "one" is conceived as opposed to the many and as the principle of all multiplicity.[19] From the point of view of traversing the Path, these two correspond to the stations of Two Bows' Length, within which the principle of many-ness is included, and Or Nearer, within which many-ness is effaced.

The relation of the things to the One can be understood through the relationship of the numerals to the number "one." Through the unity of multiplicity, or numerical oneness, the One acts as the Source for all things. All numbers are produced by a repetition of

COMMENTARY

"one." But if the One Itself manifests Itself in Its true Oneness, nothing else exists.

Finally, 'Iraqi states that the nature of God's Oneness can be grasped through our own oneness. If we turn toward Him through the unity of our own selves, we will not be faced with a duality of us and Him. Rather, the one theophany—ourselves—will be seen to be identical with the One Source of theophany. 'Iraqi's formula to explain Unity depends on the idea, greatly stressed by Ibn al-'Arabi and his followers, that each numeral reflects Unity through its uniqueness. So six is "one" because there are not two sixes; forty-seven is "one" because there are not two forty-sevens, and so forth.

FLASH XV

According to Ibn al-'Arabi and his followers, God's "Command" (*amr*) is in fact two Commands: the "prescriptive" (*taklifi*) and the "generating" (*takwini*). Through the first God sets down laws and injunctions for men to follow. In other words, He commands them to obey the prophets and follow religion. Through the second, He bestows existence on the whole of creation. "His Command, when He desires a thing, is to say to it 'Be!' and it is" (XXXVI:82). In this Flash 'Iraqi discusses the Generating Command and the fact that, from this point of view, every existent thing achieves its own special felicity as a matter of course. For all things exist only to manifest the Divine Names and Attributes. Each thing is a locus-of-manifestation for a certain ontological perfection. It cannot help but manifest its own "Lord," that is, the Name for which it acts as a locus-of-theophany. In this sense, every existent thing is on a "straight path," for each thing follows its own Lord. In the words of the Koran, "God created you and what you do" (XXXVII:96). So the creatures and all their acts are manifestations of the Generating Command.

'Iraqi explains the reason for the perfection of all existence from this point of view with his words, "Reality is a sphere. . . ." Wherever we look in existence, there is nothing but Being, Reality Itself. "Whithersoever you turn, there is the Face of God" (II:115). Each existent manifests a Name, so each is nothing but the Being that is named. So the things do not differ among themselves inasmuch as they are Being's loci-of-manifestation. "Thou seest not in the creation of the All-Merciful any disparity" (LXVII:3). In Qunawi's words,

COMMENTARY

"There is no difference between God's Attentiveness toward bestowing existence upon the Throne and the Supreme Pen on the one hand, and His Attentiveness toward bestowing existence upon an ant on the other—in respect of the Unity of His Essence and the Attentiveness."[20]

Although here 'Iraqi does not refer to the complementary teaching, that is, the nature and function of the Prescriptive Command, that has always been obvious enough to people who live in a society where all public and private activities are governed by the normative directives of Revelation. In any case, the importance of the Prescriptive Command is discussed thoroughly by Ibn al-'Arabi and his followers, and 'Iraqi alludes to it in Flash XXI.

It is true that each thing's "felicity" is to follow its own Lord and to realize that which coincides with its own reality or archetypal-entity. In other words, a thing's felicity is its ultimate end, which is to display the Name it manifests. But there is a tremendous difference between the properties of a Name like "All-Merciful" or "Forgiving" on the one hand, and Names such as "He-who-leads-astray" and "Avenger" on the other. The entity's felicity may in fact be wretchedness and damnation from the human point of view. The only path open to man in order for him to attain the felicity and mercy that pertain to the "Benevolent Names" (al-asma' al-lutfiyyah) and to avoid the wretchedness and wrath that are manifested by the "All-Subjugating Names" (al-asma' al-qahriyyah) is to follow the Divine Law.

One of the functions of the Prescriptive Command is to separate those human beings who have the capacity to act as loci-of-theophany for God's Benevolent Names from those who manifest His All-Subjugating Names. Thus "heaven" and "hell" remain very real, since they are the ultimate result of this separation and differentiation. In any case, since God has commanded the servant to follow His prescriptions and directives, he has no choice but to try to do so, whether or not he succeeds.[21]

FLASH XVI

In this Flash 'Iraqi explains again through further images that all things are the Self-Manifestations of Being and that all acts are His, since He is the One Agent. And since He performs all acts, He also "forgives" them, since the acts cannot really be attributed to the creatures. They are veils hiding His perfection. Thus, even those entities that manifest His Wrathful and All-Subjugating Names are embraced by His Mercy, for, according to the *hadith qudsi*, "My Mercy precedes My Wrath." Hence the Prophet said, "There will come a time upon hell when watercress grows from its deepest pit."[22]

FLASH XVII

'Iraqi has not so far paid particular attention to the role of the entity in God's Self-Manifestation. In this Flash he discusses the entity in detail in keeping with the terminology of Ibn al-'Arabi's school.

To follow 'Iraqi's discussion, we must remember the two fundamental theophanies of Being. The first, which is synonymous with the First Entification, is called the "Most Holy Effusion" or the "Unseen Theophany." Through it God manifests Himself to Himself in Himself. All the possibilities of ontological unfolding latent within the Hidden Treasure are witnessed by God at the level of His Knowledge. In other words, the immutable archetypal-entities—the "realities" or "meanings"—become entified within the Unseen. Here also the "universal preparedness" of the entities is determined, that is, their capacity to act as receptacles for Being.[23] Hence at this first stage the degree to which each entity will be able to display the infinite perfections of Nondelimited Being is determined. But the entity remains totally "nonexistent."

The second theophany is called the "Holy Effusion" or the "Visible Theophany." Through it being is bestowed on each entity in keeping with its universal preparedness. As a result, creation as such takes place: all the ontological-levels and the existent-entities within them become outwardly manifest. At this stage the "particular preparedness" comes into play. It determines to what extent each individual entity can act as a receptacle for Nonentified Being and Its perfection at each instant or stage in the entity's becoming.

But the particular preparedness is determined by the universal preparedness, just as the Holy Effusion is determined by the Most Holy Effusion. The difference between the two preparednesses may be said to consist in "summated-unity" and "particularized-deployment." At the level of the Most Holy Effusion all the ontological perfections that will be displayed by each entity are known by God at once within His One Knowledge. But at the level of the Holy Effu-

COMMENTARY

sion, these perfections become strung out one after another in a chain of cause and effect, so each existent-entity manifests its inherent perfections only gradually.

'Iraqi begins by discussing the lover's particular preparedness in his journey to God. As the lover progresses, his ontological perfections are brought one by one from potentiality to actuality. His particular preparedness gradually broadens in scope, since each perfection he actualizes prepares him for actualizing still greater perfections. But the more perfections of Sheer Being that he embraces, the more he grasps and understands. For the more he partakes of Being, the more his knowledge increases, since knowledge is one of Being's primary perfections.[24] The more his knowledge increases, the more he becomes aware of his own ignorance and the fact that his finite perfections are literally nothing in the face of Being's infinite perfections. In fact, his perfections do not even belong to him, they pertain to God alone. So the more he progresses, the more the gap between him and God seems to widen. Finally he must abandon his own selfhood and attain annihilation in God. Only then can duality be effaced and true perfection be realized.

Having discussed the role of the particular preparedness in allowing man to return to his Origin, 'Iraqi then wants to forestall any misunderstanding. Certain people might think that the particular preparedness really belongs to the entity. But in fact, like the Being for which it acts as a receptacle, it also derives from the One, that is, at the stage of the Most Holy Effusion. First the lover must receive a glimmer of His Light (= entification of the universal preparedness within Knowledge). Only then can he contemplate His Beauty and act as a receptacle for His perfections. In every case the advances the lover makes on the Path have already been preceded by God's bestowal of preparedness on him in his state of nonexistence in God's Knowledge. It is always God's "initiative" at the level of the archetypal-entity that allows the lover to pass on to greater and greater ontological perfections. But from the point of view of the individual in the world and his particular preparedness, each advance makes him ready for a further advance.

Finally, 'Iraqi interprets the sayings of some early Sufis in the light of Ibn al-'Arabi's teachings. And he points out that the preparedness of the Perfect Man is in fact unlimited. Since the Perfect Men are mirrors for Nondelimited Being as such, they never cease experiencing Its theophanies. They never come to rest at any fixed station. No one should imagine that because he has finished the journey *to* God, the journey *in* God has also come to an end, or will ever come to an end.

FLASH XVIII

In this Flash 'Iraqi again refers to Love as the motivating force of all creation. It was Love that brought the creatures out from their state of latency and nonexistence within the Hidden Treasure. And it is this same Love that makes manifest all the possibilities inherent within Infinite Being and therefore brings about all the commotion and excitement known as the "world."

In this discussion, 'Iraqi alludes to one of the favorite teachings of his master, Qunawi: All the cosmos is a great Book and everything that exists along with all that sleeps within nonexistence can be described by the image of letters, words, and sentences.[25] As Jami explains in his commentary on this section, each atom or each thing is an ontological "word." And "if the sea were ink for the words of my Lord, the sea would be spent before the words of my Lord are spent, though We brought replenishment the like of it" (XVIII:10). Each word is the locus-of-manifestation for a Divine Name. Each Name has a specific tongue through which it expresses the Divine Mysteries and tells of the perfections of Being. Each tongue has a peculiar speech through which it manifests these Mysteries. And the true lover has an ear directed toward each and every word, for he is the Perfect Man who acts as a mirror for all of God's perfections. But ultimately, the lover himself is none but the Beloved.

FLASH XIX

Only the Perfect Man possesses the Heart about which God said in the *hadith qudsi*, "My heaven embraces Me not, nor My earth, but the Heart of My believing, gentle and meek servant does embrace Me." To attain such a Heart is the goal of the Path.[26] In Qunawi's words, "As for the scope of the Heart which embraces God, it is the scope of the Isthmus-Nature which pertains exclusively to the True Man."[27] As the "Isthmus of Isthmuses," the Perfect Man comprehends all the Presences and stands on the Point of Equilibrium at the Center of the Circle of Being.[28] In him and in him alone are all of God's perfections reflected in their full splendor and amplitude, without any intermediary. Since he stands next to God, he is the isthmus between Him and all of creation and the means whereby existence becomes deployed among all the entities.

The Perfect Man as the immediate Self-Manifestation of God displays His Absolute Unity. In Qunawi's terms, he is the "One Effusion from the One." The world as such could never be created by God as such, since "None issues from the One but One." But since the Perfect Man displays God's Oneness in his own oneness, he becomes the cause of a certain duality between himself and God. On the basis of this duality, multiplicity can come into existence. All God's Names and Attributes, which are displayed in a unitary mode within the Perfect Man's oneness, become differentiated within him so that each requires a separate locus-of-manifestation. So the Perfect Man is the ontological nexus between God and the world. He is the Isthmus that separates the two sides and that possesses the attributes of both.

'Iraqi's discussion in this Flash centers on the Perfect Man and his infinite Heart, which is his reality and the locus in which he acts as intermediary between God and the world. Only the oneness of this Heart can be a mirror for God's Oneness. In fact, the Heart is uncreated, for creation begins only *after* the effusion of the Perfect Man's reality, which is the very entification of Knowledge within God. In other words, it is the Most Holy Effusion and the station of Two Bows' Length, or even that of Or Nearer. The reality of the Perfect Man, his Heart, is nothing but God's Face turned toward the bestowal of existence on the world. Qunawi even states that the Station of Divinity—that is, God envisaged as comprehending all the Names and Attributes and as Lord of the Worlds—is one of the ontological levels that belong to the Perfect Man.[29] Only the Nonentified Essence is beyond him.

FLASH XX

The Beloved, or the Necessary-Being, is the source of all perfections and all existence; whereas the lover, the possible-existent, has nothing of his own. The reality of the lover pertains to "nonexistence"—his entification within Knowledge—since Being belongs only to God. So man's perfection lies in his true state, nonexistence, or, from the point of view of the Path, "poverty," which has always been a synonym for Sufism. Through it man "delivers his trust—existence—back to its owner" and returns to his Source. Hence the goal

COMMENTARY

of the wayfarer is "annihilation," through which the lover's false ascription of things and attributes to himself is effaced. He understands
and realizes in every dimension of his own entification that only God
is.

On the basis of this perspective concerning man's fundamental
nature, 'Iraqi considers a number of definitions the Sufis have given
for the "poor man" and "poverty" and shows how we can discern
within them various levels of perfection.

Jami comments on the saying "Poverty is intrinsic need . . ." as
follows: "Since the poor-man strives only to attain Absolute Reality,
and since It has no special relationship with any specific entification,
each thing (i.e., each entity) is equal in the Sufi's eye. He needs every
one of them in respect of the Self-Manifestation of that Reality within
it. But no entification's specific quality enters into that need."

Concerning the beginning of the last paragraph Jami writes,
" 'Know that the rich man for the most part is far' in respect to meaning, since the substance of proximity is Annihilation, but that cannot
be joined with wealth and relationships, except rarely in the case of
certain Perfect Men—hence he said 'for the most part'—'in the extremity of nearness' in respect to appearances, for he is clothed in various signs of proximity. But 'the poor-man is always near,' since
hindrances have been removed, and the fact that he is empty of relationships aids him in realizing proximity 'in the extremity of farness'
in respect to his outward form, since he is clothed in the signs of farness."

FLASH XXI

In order to attain the goal of the Path, the wayfarer must undergo the annihilation of his own attributes. In an immediate, practical
sense, before the lover has advanced on the Way, this means that he
must submit his will to God. Only by giving up his own desires can
he truly follow God's Desire. We cannot even argue that the "lover
should aspire toward perfection," since as long as the *lover* is aspiring
toward perfection, this bespeaks his own egocentricity, his own sepa-
rative and illusory existence. Ultimately man must abandon all
things, including himself.

The first thing implied by the lover's "submission to God's Will"
(= *islam*) is that he must follow the revealed Law (*Shari'ah*). Religion
is the manifestation of God's Will and Desire for man in the form of

teachings that govern every dimension of man's life. Only by turning to His revelation—His "Prescriptive Command" (Flash XV)—can man understand what God wants and does not want from him. So in all his activities the lover must view the injunctions of the Shari'ah as his basic guide. What the Shari'ah forbids is to be avoided, for the lover does not want to attract the Beloved's disapproval and censure to himself. He must seek to approach the Beloved by acting in accordance with His Will, not to remain distant from Him by acting contrary to it.

Someone may argue that the world is the Self-Manifestation of God. When man sees God in all things, how can he distinguish between this and that? How can he say that "such a thing is good" and "such a thing is bad"? But this argument is misleading. It is true that all that exists, by the very fact of existence, partakes of God's Being, His Essence. This is what is meant when it is said that everything follows God's Generating Command. For the existent things and all their properties and acts are the unfolding of the possibilities of manifestation latent within Nonentified Being.

But man cannot avoid taking the Prescriptive Command into account, and at this level he will contemplate the theophany of God's Names and Attributes, not His Essence. The reason for this is as follows: Individual man is potentially the Perfect Man, which means that his *reality* is the One Effusion from the One. In other terms, the "human reality" may be said to be the Name "Allah," the All-Comprehensive Name that embraces all other Names. This is why God says about Adam, the prototype of man and the first Perfect Man on the earth, "He taught Adam the Names, all of them" (II:31). As a result, man is a central creature, and the Perfect Man is the Central Presence. Fundamentally, "centrality" means that the relationship of man to each one of the Names is equal to his relationship with every other. As the Self-Manifestation of Nonentified Being as such, man is not delimited by any Name representing a particular ontological perfection. On the contrary, he is the locus-of-manifestation for the Name that manifests Being *qua* Being. This is why Qunawi calls the Perfect Man who has realized this station the "Point at the Center of the Circle." He is situated at the dead center of Being envisaged as a Circle within which all Its perfections—all the Names, all the entities—are deployed. Like Being Itself, the Perfect Man can assume any entification without becoming delimited by it.

COMMENTARY

Because of his centrality, man is set apart from all other existents, each of which is peripheral in some respect. Thus the angels manifest only certain Divine Names. As a result they say, "None of us there is, but has a known station" (XXXVII:164). For the same reason, God commanded them to bow down to Adam (II:34). And He showed them Adam's superiority over them by demonstrating to them that they knew only their *own* Names—that is, the Names of Being for which they acted as loci-of-manifestation—not the Names of other than themselves. "Glory be to Thee! We know not but what Thou hast taught us!" (II:32). In a similar way, all other creatures but man are peripheral and manifest only certain Names of God.

So man's superiority lies in his knowledge of all the Names—that is, in the fact that he manifests all ontological perfections. Since the most important of these perfections are Life, Knowledge, Will, and Power,[30] man *lives* in the world, has *knowledge* of his own situation, can exercise his *will* to choose between possibilities of action, and has the *power* to carry out his choice. Because he is a "transcription of Being," he possesses all Its Attributes. In other words, he lives, knows, chooses, and acts whether he wants to or not.

Man cannot ignore his own nature. To do so would be to deny his own humanity, or, in Koranic language, "to refuse to carry the Trust." Man is forced to choose and act on the basis of his knowledge by his very nature. And since his knowledge is limited—as long as he is not the Perfect Man—he needs guidance to ensure that he makes the right choices. He must follow the Prescriptive Command.

In short, only man is given the capacity to act as a receptacle for all of Being's perfections. Thus potentially he is situated at the Point at the Center of the Circle, equidistant from each perfection. But only the Perfect Men truly realize this station. In practice, other men are dominated by one of the Names, and thus they leave "Equilibrium" and gravitate toward the periphery.

In order to attain the station of Centrality, Equilibrium, and Perfection, man must have a perfect affinity for Being as such, or, in other words, he must employ the ontological perfections that he has already actualized in the manner in which Being as such by Its very nature demands. This is the only way he can employ his particular preparedness to achieve even greater preparednesses and to ascend toward his goal. And since man is imprisoned within the limitations of the World of Corporeal-Bodies, the nature of Sheer Being can be clarified only by Being Itself through Its Speech (another one of Its basic perfections[31]), that is, Its Prescriptive Command. Unaided, man is caught in the corporeal world and cut off from the inward dimensions of his reality. His very *raison d'être* is to actualize the potential perfections hidden within himself. And he cannot actualize the perfection of Outwardness without himself dwelling within it. But once there, the Inward must guide him back to Itself.

So the lover who is seeking to actualize the station of the Perfect Man must avoid disequilibrium and the properties of the Names that bring about distance from the Center—the All-Subjugating and Wrathful Names. He must strive for proximity to the Benevolent and Merciful Names. And here we should mention that Ibn al-'Arabi and his followers identify "Wrath" with nonexistence and "Mercy" with Being. So "to seek refuge in God's Mercy" is to return to Being Itself.[32]

In this Flash 'Iraqi alludes to the Generating Command as the "Theophany of the Essence." But man's centrality does not allow him to ignore the theophanies of the Names and Attributes. Since he has been given the special station of being able to differentiate among all the Names, he has no choice but to choose between their properties. It is true that all things are theophanies of the Essence, but they are also theophanies of the Names and Attributes. The Prescriptive Command gives man the key with which to discern among the theophanies of the different Names and to choose those that will aid him in his return to his Source, the Central Presence.

By his very nature as a transcription of Being man understands that things become manifested in keeping with the Names and Attributes, whose properties are diverse. So he must remember the Prophet's prayer: "I seek refuge in Thy Forgiveness from Thy Punishment, I seek refuge in Thy Approval from Thy Anger, I seek refuge in Thee from Thee." Man cannot count a theophany of God's Wrath as equivalent to one of His Mercy. The locus-of-manifestation for the Name "He-who-leads-astray" cannot evoke within him the same reaction as the locus for the Name "He-who-guides." Even in the case of the theophany of the Essence Itself—which might make us fear that the Generating Command was in conflict with the Prescriptive Command—man can seek refuge from Him in Him. "So flee to God!" (LI:50).

COMMENTARY

FLASH XXII

As 'Iraqi has already pointed out, the annihilation of selfhood and the attributes of possible-existence, so that only the Necessary-Being remains, demands among other things that the lover completely abandon his own desires. Here 'Iraqi develops this theme further, showing that submission to the Will of the Beloved implies certain things that one might not suspect at the outset. For it means that the lover must not desire Union with the Beloved, a Union that would seem to be the whole motivation for entering on the Path. But in fact, as long as the lover-Beloved duality subsists, man remains far from True Oneness, which is Love and Love alone.

When the lover desires something, he always has a delimited and defined goal in mind. His desire is not for God as such, who is Nonentified and therefore Unknowable and even Undesirable. The realization of perfection implies that all the lover's attributes have been annihilated and effaced in God. At the highest station, it means that man is not drawn toward the property of any Name or Attribute—or any entification. Rather, he remains nondelimited as the Point at the Center of the Circle.

So the lover must surrender his own desires to those of the Beloved. So much is this so that he must be happy with separation from his Desire, as long as he knows that this is what the Beloved wants. Going even farther than this, 'Iraqi then says that in fact separation is more desirable than Union. But again he qualifies his words, stating that the separation he means is that desired by God, while the Union is that desired by man.

Finally 'Iraqi refers to the station where the lover realizes that everything he manifests and everything he is derives from the Beloved. But again, 'Iraqi makes clear that he is not speaking about just anyone who might understand this principle mentally or imagine falsely that he has actualized it. For he says, "a lover who is qualified by the Beloved's attributes," and as Jami points out, this is a reference to the Proximity of Supererogatory-Works, the first station of the Perfect Man. At this level the wayfarer has already attained Union and travels from Attribute to Attribute.[33] But the traveler who is still imperfect and aspires to reach his station may still take him as his model.

159

COMMENTARY

FLASH XXIII

This Flash develops the theme of the previous Flash, that the ultimate goal is not the Beloved, but Love Itself. As long as the lover loves the Beloved, duality remains. The level where the Names and Attributes are differentiated from one another cannot be transcended. In other words, the very highest station that can have been attained is that of Two Bows' Length. At the station of Or Nearer, only God remains.

In the last section, beginning with the words "Look still higher" (i.e., from the lover to the Beloved), 'Iraqi interprets the Koranic verse "He has forgotten them" to mean that the Beloved Himself is annihilated in Love, the Nondelimited Essence, for all Names and Attributes are negated; there is no outward-manifestation (lover) or inward-nonmanifestation (Beloved), only the One.

FLASH XXIV

Being belongs to God, whereas nonexistence is the inherent quality of the creature. Even though Qunawi and his followers often speak of the archetypal-entity acting as a "receptacle" for Being, or employ other such images that imply the existence of the entity, the truth of the matter is that "the entity has never smelt the fragrance of existence." The entity is always inward and nonmanifest, since it does not exist.

To review an image to which we have already referred, Being is Light, while the entities are darkness. Only the effects of the entities become manifest, not they themselves, which means that darkness mixed with Light results in "brightness" (diya'),[34] or the dimming of the Light. By acting as a veil over Sheer Light, darkness allows the myriad colors—or possibilities and perfections of outward manifestation latent within the very nature of Light—to be perceived. But what becomes outward and visible is never anything other than Light, for darkness has no positive reality and thus can never itself be seen. The nature of the varying degrees of "brightness" that are perceived is not determined by darkness, but by the essence of Light itself. In other words, the very nature of the creatures that become outwardly manifest through the Holy Effusion is determined by the Most Holy Effusion that preceded it, an Effusion that represents the delineation of the possible perfections of manifestation inherent within Nonentified Being.

FLASH XXV

Following the Koranic terminology, the Sufis divide certainty into three stages: the Knowledge of Certainty, the Eye of Certainty, and the Truth of Certainty.[35] The Knowledge of Certainty is as if one were to be convinced, through rational proofs, that fire exists. The Eye of Certainty is to see the fire. The Truth of Certainty is to be consumed by it. Here 'Iraqi begins with the lover or the person who is already an aspirant on the Path. He began his Wayfaring because of his certainty concerning the existence of the Beloved and the necessity of seeking Him. The Path of course is long. In the words of Awhaduddin Kirmani, "Unless your heart and eyes bleed with longing (and aspiration) for fifty years, you will never be shown the way from words to spiritual states."[36]

But then one day, after long travail, the lover sees the Beloved. Moreover, he realizes that he had always seen Him, but he had not been aware that he was seeing Him. For everyone sees the Beloved, since only He exists. Then the lover comprehends the Truth of Certainty, he is annihilated in the Beloved; and lover, Beloved, and Love are One.

FLASH XXVI

In this Flash 'Iraqi considers some of the consequences of the duality necessitated by the fact that the lover and the Beloved possess a real differentiation stemming from the First Entification. This distinction between the two of them manifests itself in different ways at various stages of the Path. In fact the lover must exist before the attributes of Belovedness can make themselves manifest. In other words, without the world, the Name-derived Perfection cannot be displayed. If there were no "others," the mutually opposing properties required by many of the Names would be effaced by Oneness. When opposites coincide in every respect, they are no longer opposites. If they never separate and make their opposition manifest, it is meaningless to speak of them as "opposites."

In the first paragraph, 'Iraqi alludes to the Self-Manifestation of

COMMENTARY

God within all Presences. Only the Perfect Man in his All-Comprehensiveness possesses the capacity to contemplate God at every one of these levels. In fact, God's "Face" turned toward each level is the face of the Perfect Man turned toward Him, for between God and the Perfect Man there is no intermediary. Hence Qunawi says that the Heart of the Perfect Man, the Heart that embraces God, has five faces:

"(1) A face turned toward the Presence of God, with no intermediary between Him and it. (2) A face standing opposite the World of the Spirits, through which man takes from his Lord, through the intermediary of the Spirits, what his preparedness allows. (3) A face pertaining to the World of Image-Exemplars.... (4) A face adjacent to the World of Sensory-Perception and pertaining to the Names 'Outward' and 'Last.' (5) An all-comprehensive face pertaining exclusively to the Unity of All-Comprehensiveness. Adjacent to this Unity lies the 'He-ness' described by Firstness, Lastness, Outwardness, Inwardness and the Comprehension of these four descriptions."[37] In other words, this last face gazes on the Divine Essence or "He-ness" about which God says, "*He* is the First and the Last and the Outward and the Inward" (LVII:3). (In contrast, the first face gazes on the First Entification, the Presence of Knowledge.)

FLASH XXVII

Annihilation of the lover's attributes and existence, which brings about subsistence within the Beloved, is nothing but the lover's return to his own Source. For in himself he is nonexistence: Being belongs to God and God alone. As long as he dwells in the illusion of selfhood and his own existentiality, he is far from the Truth. But "Truth will come, and falsehood will vanish away" (XVII:81). The reality and felicity of the lover lie in his return to his origin, nonexistence. Then only can he realize that he is one of the myriad Perfections of Nonentified Being and as such, he is none other than the Beloved.

FLASH XXVIII

In this Flash 'Iraqi alludes to two of his master's important teachings: the "spiritual-ascent of decomposition" and the "Specific Face."[38] Man is the "all-comprehensive isthmus" who embraces the

COMMENTARY

Sea of Necessary-Being and the Sea of Possible-Existence. He contains all the perfections of Sheer Being, whether they pertain to God and the Inward or to the world and the Outward. But to realize these perfections and become the Perfect Man, within whom all ontological potentialities are actualized, man must dwell within each ontological level and Presence and acquire its peculiar perfections. Of course at the level of his reality—his archetypal-entity—man already possesses each level's perfections as his own. When we look more closely, we see that the Presences are nothing but the outward manifestation of his own ontological potentialities. But to actualize these potentialities, man must journey through the worlds and Presences. He must acquire all the attributes and properties that the worlds make manifest.

Man's journey through the worlds is called the "spiritual-ascent of composition" ('uruj at-tarkib), even though outwardly it appears to be a descent. Through it man descends from inward nonmanifestation within Knowledge to outward manifestation within the world. First he descends to the Universal Intellect (= the Supreme Pen), then to the Universal Soul (= the Guarded Tablet). These are the two extremes of the World of the Spirits. Within this world he acquires an outward spiritual existence and thereby begins to be compounded from various ontological perfections. Then he passes into the World of Image-Exemplars, which extends from the Tablet to the Throne. Within this world he acquires the perfections of psychic and imaginal existence. Then man enters the World of Corporeal-Bodies, which extends from the Throne (= the starless heaven), to the Footstool (= the heaven of the fixed stars), through the remaining seven heavens, and finally to the earth, the elements and the three kingdoms. As he travels, man acquires the perfection of all these levels. Finally he reaches the human state in the world. This is the farthest limit of the spiritual-ascent of composition.

Of course one must be careful not to imagine some sort of physical journey by man through the worlds. As Qunawi explains, man's journey is "supraformal," which means it relates to his "meaning" or immutable archetypal-entity. The various worlds and levels man "passes through" are from another point of view the realities that the human reality embraces and that unfold in stages as the Hidden Treasure attains the Perfection of Distinct-Manifestation.

So when man is born into the world, he finishes the spiritual-ascent of composition. Through it he has left the First Presence, passed

COMMENTARY

through the Worlds of Spirits and of Image-Exemplars, and entered into the Corporeal World. As a man within this world he has now reached the first stage of the fifth and Central Presence, that of the Perfect Man. He now embraces all kinds of existence, as well as nonexistence, within himself. Now he must actualize his potentialities and consciously integrate the four Presences that preceded him into the All-Comprehensive Presence. He must perfect the human state, within which these multiple Presences may return to Unity.

Having reached the human level, man begins the "spiritual-ascent of decomposition" (mi'raj at-tahlil). Through it he reascends to his origin, the state of nonexistence within Knowledge. At each level he passes, he returns what he had acquired in his descent to its owner. This is the "journey to God." Having reached its end, man has now actualized all the Presences, he has comprehended their many-ness in his own oneness. They had become manifested from his all-comprehensive reality in the first place, and now they return to nonexistence within his reality. Here man reaches the first station of the Perfect Man. Between him and God there is now no intermediary. On the one hand there is God, and on the other there is the Perfect Man, the One who had issued from the One, who has now returned to the One, and who has integrated all many-ness into God. Within him the four Presences other than himself are deployed as so many dimensions of the Central and All-Comprehensive Presence. He has passed through the reality of each of them, actualized it within himself, and returned it to Unity.

Before his "ascent" into composition, all the ontological perfections are potentialities of outward manifestation latent within his own reality. Having traversed the Circle of Being, man actualizes these perfections, manifests the Hidden Treasure and comes to know Nonentified Being in Its full deployment. When man reaches this station, God decides whether or not to return him to the world in order to be a guide for others. In Qunawi's words, "If God now wants him to return to the World of the Visible in order to bring about the perfection of others, or himself (i.e., so that he may attain even higher stations of Perfection related to the Outward), or both together, man will return (to the Visible World) by undergoing a supra-formal composition after Opening (i.e., after having attained Union). This composition corresponds to his decomposition (which he underwent during his spiritual-ascent)."[39] But now man subsists within God, so

COMMENTARY

his attributes are direct and conscious manifestations of God's Attributes.

As for the "Specific Face" (al-wajh al-khass), this is the Face of God turned toward and specific to every created existent. Between each thing and the Specific Face God turns toward it there is no intermediary, although in other respects there are numerous intermediaries between it and God. Ultimately, this "Face" is the thing's entification within God's Knowledge. It is the immutable archetypal-entity, which, like the Knowledge of which it is the object, is eternal.

Through his return to his own Specific Face, which is his source, man attains his everlasting felicity. Only this archetypal-entity subsists; all else is man's outward form, the manifestation of his entity's properties. So all else perishes.

Not only man, but each and every thing has a Specific Face turned toward it, an entification within Knowledge. To know things "as they are" is to know them in God as He knows them. This is the knowledge of the Specific Faces of the things, a knowledge attained only by the Perfect Men.

NOTES

1. See Jami's commentary on this section of the *Lama'at*; also Jami, *Sharh-i ruba'iyyat*, ed. M. Hirawi (Kabul, 1343/1964), pp. 40–41.

2. Qunawi quotes this verse in *Matali'-i iman*, ed. W. C. Chittick, *Sophia Perennis IV*, no. 1 (Spring 1978), 57–80 (Persian section) (p. 80); translated in *Ascendant Stars*.

3. See *Ascendant Stars*: ALL-SUBJUGATING-POWER, RESURRECTION.

4. See *Miftah al-ghayb*, pp. 301–302; *Ashi''at al-lama'at*, pp. 15–16. Ibn al-'Arabi often refers to the two lower stations. See for example, Chittick, "Ibn 'Arabi's own Summary," I, no. 2: 114–116.

5. See Ahmad-i Jam, *Rawdat al-mudhannibin*, ed. A. Fadil (Tehran, 1355/1976), pp. 218, 314–316.

6. See *Ascendant Stars*: UNVEILING, ANNIHILATION.

7. *Al-Futuhat al-makkiyyah*, 4 vols. (Beirut, n.d.), vol. 4, pp. 202–203.

8. See *an-Nusus*, p. 299/215–216; *Naqd an-nusus*, pp. 47–48; also Chittick, "Sadr al-Din Qunawi on the Oneness of Being," pp. 181ff.

9. The "entity" or "quiddity" is contrasted with Being and represents one of Its perfections. Only Being as such has no quiddity. But Qunawi writes about the highest station of man's perfection: "Its possessor has no entity" (*an-Nafahat al-ilahiyyah*, p. 305).

COMMENTARY

10. See Farghani's discussion of the difference between theophany and incarnation, or between unification in its allowed and disallowed senses, in *Mashariq ad-darari*, pp. 271–273; also *Ascendant Stars:* UNIFICATION.

11. See *Ascendant Stars:* OPENING.

12. See *Ascendant Stars:* BEWILDERMENT; also T. Izutsu, "The Concept of Perpetual Creation in Islamic Mysticism and Zen Buddhism," in S. H. Nasr, *Mélanges offerts à Henry Corbin* (Tehran, 1977), especially pp. 136ff.

13. See *Ascendant Stars:* VEIL; also F. Schuon, "Le mystère du voile," *Sophia Perennis* II, no. 2 (Autumn 1976), pp. 7–21.

14. See *Mashariq ad-darari*, pp. 19, 186, 312–313, 492, 494, 637, 646.

15. *Tahrir al-bayan fi taqrir shu'ab al-iman*, Mss. Crh. 2054, Fatih 1394, 2630, Şehid Ali Paşa 1340, Halet Ef. ilavesi 66 (Süleymaniye Library, Istanbul). Farghani has a similar discussion in *Muntaha-l-madarik* (Istanbul, 1293/1876), p. 13; quoted in *Naqd an-nusus*, pp. 36–37.

16. See *Ascendant Stars:* CIRCLE, PRESENCE.

17. *Muntaha-l-madarik*, p. 13; *Naqd an-nusus*, p. 37.

18. *Fusus al-hikam*, ed. A. 'Afifi (Beirut, 1946), p. 105.

19. See *an-Nusus*, p. 294/209; *I'jaz al-bayan*, pp. 115–118/224–226; cf. *al-Fukuk*, pp. 233–234.

20. *I'jaz al-bayan*, p. 290/408; quoted in *Naqd an-nusus*, p. 185.

21. See *Naqd an-nusus*, pp. 167–168, 172–176, 183–193; cf. "Ibn 'Arabi's own Summary" I, no. 2: 120–122.

22. *Naqd an-nusus*, p. 190. On hell's limited nature, see ibid., pp. 188–190.

23. See *Ascendant Stars:* PREPAREDNESS.

24. Ibid.: RECEPTACLE.

25. See for example *I'jaz al-bayan*, pp. 85–86/193–194; *an-Nafahat al-ilahiyyah*, p. 81; *Miftah al-ghayb*, pp. 271–274.

26. See *Ascendant Stars:* HEART.

27. *Al-Fukuk*, p. 250; quoted in *Naqd an-nusus*, p. 202.

28. See Commentary on Flash XXI; also *Ascendant Stars:* CIRCLE, EQUILIBRIUM.

29. *An-Nafahat al-ilahiyyah*, p. 84.

30. Qunawi calls these Names the "Four Pillars of Divinity" (*chahar rukn-i uluhiyyat*) in his Persian works, and in his Arabic works refers to them as the first manifestation of the "Keys to the Unseen" (the Unfathomable Names of God), "which none knows but He" (VI:59). His work *Miftah al-ghayb* ("The Key to the Unseen") discusses them thoroughly.

31. It is the fifth or the seventh of the "Seven Leaders" (*al-a'immat as-sab'ah*), the seven primary Names of God. See *Naqd an-nusus*, pp. 40–42.

32. See *Ascendant Stars:* MERCY.

33. *Miftah al-ghayb*, p. 302.

34. See *al-Fukuk*, p. 223; *Naqd an-nusus*, p. 178.

35. See A. Siraj al-Din, *The Book of Certainty* (London, 1952).

COMMENTARY

36. Quoted by Qunawi in *Tabsirat al-mubtadi'*.

37. *Al-Fukuk*, pp. 246–247; quoted in *Naqd an-nusus*, p. 200.

38. Qunawi develops these teachings extensively in *Miftah al-ghayb*, especially pp. 294–304; see also *I'jaz al-bayan*, pp. 336–342/458–464.

39. *Miftah al-ghayb*, p. 296.

Selected Bibliography

Bell, J. N.: *Love Theory in Later Ḥanbalite Islam,* Albany, 1979 (Illustrates in a scholarly manner the intellectual background of the discussion of love in Islam and alludes to the views of various Sufis).

Burckhardt, T.: An *Introduction to Sufi Doctrine,* Lahore, 1959 (An excellent introduction to Ibn al-'Arabi's teachings).

————*Wisdom of the Prophets,* translated from French by A. Culme-Seymour, Gloucestershire, 1975 (Partial translation of Ibn al'Arabi's *Fusus al-ḥikam*).

Corbin, H.: *Creative Imagination in the Ṣūfism of Ibn 'Arabī,* translated from the French by R. Manheim, Princeton, 1969 (Important study of one aspect of Ibn al-'Arabi's thought and its wider implications).

Izutsu, T.: *A Comparative Study of the Key Philosophical Concepts in Sufism and Taoism—Ibn 'Arabī and Lao-Tzŭ, Chuang-Tzŭ,* two parts, Tokyo, 1966 (The best study in a European language of the ideas of Ibn al-'Arabi).

Nasr, S. H.: *Sufi Essays,* London, 1972; Albany, 1973 (Excellent study of various dimensions of Sufism and its relevance to modern life).

————*Three Muslim Sages,* Harvard (Mass.), 1964 (Best summary of the life, work, thought and importance of Ibn al-'Arabi).

Nicholson, R.A.: *Studies in Islamic Mysticism,* Cambridge, 1921; first paperback edition, 1978 (Contains an important study of Jili, one of Ibn al-'Arabi's most famous followers).

————*The Tarjumān al-Ashwāq, A Collection of Mystical Odes by Muḥyi'ddīn ibn al-'Arabī,* London, 1911; reprinted 1978 (A translation of poems on love with Ibn al-'Arabi's own commentary).

Pourjavady, N. and Wilson, P.L.: *Kings of Love, The History and Poetry of the Ni'matullāhī Sufi Order of Iran,* Tehran, 1978 (The 600-year history of a Sufi order which has continued the tradition represented by 'Iraqi to the present day; includes more than fifty pages of translated poetry).

BIBLIOGRAPHY

Schuon, F.: *Dimensions of Islam*, London, 1970 (Besides illuminating remarks on Sufism the work contains a discussion of the earthly concomitants of the love of God in the Sufi perspective).

————*Understanding Islam*, London, 1963 (The best study of the role of Sufism in Islam).

Valiuddin, M.: *Love of God: The Sufi Approach*, New Delhi, 1968 (Wide-ranging if somewhat disorganized study).

Weischer, B. M. and Wilson, P. L.: *Heart's Witness: The Sufi Quatrains of Awḥaduddīn Kirmānī*, Tehran, 1978 (Translation of 120 quatrains by a figure whose tradition 'Iraqi continues).

Index to Preface,
Introduction,
Commentary & Notes

INDEX

INDEX

172

INDEX

INDEX

INDEX

Index to Text

INDEX

INDEX